JEREMY HARMER

MERIDIAN

Activity Book 1

Longman

Longman Group Limited
Longman House, Burnt Mill, Harlow,
Essex CM20 2JE, England

First published 1985
Second impression 1986

ISBN 0-582-57950-3

Set in 10/12 pt Univers medium, Linotron 202
Printed and bound in Spain by
TONSA, San Sebastian

Illustrated by Tony Kenyon, Charles Front, David Parkins and Jerry Collins
Cover design by Lloyd Northover

The following svmbols are used:

- pairwork
- groups of three
- groupwork
- whole class activity
- teamwork

1 Classwork

Interaction

1

Look at the pictures. Put the words below in the right speech bubbles.

(In Los Angeles.) (Hello.) (Where do you live?)

(What's your name?) (What do you do?)

2

In this game **A** shows a sequence of numbers with fingers. **B** says the numbers. **C** writes the numbers down. (*Remember*: **A** does not talk. **C** can't see **A**.)

Listening and acting out

1

Who is talking – **a**, **b** or **c**?

a Anne: housewife *Tarragona*
b James: teacher *Oxford*
c Laura: student *London*

2

Have conversations like the one on the cassette.
Student **A** is a doctor, student **B** a patient.
Student **A** should ask **B** about his/her occupation.
Student **A** fills in the following form about **B**.

NAME: ______________________

HOME: ______________________

OCCUPATION: ______________________

Language summary

New language items

What's your name?
(= What is)
– I'm [John].
(= I am)

Where do you live?
– In [London].

What do you do?
– I'm a [doctor].
(= I am)

What's yours?
What about you?

New vocabulary/expressions * Activity Book vocabulary

Places
London
New York
Paris
Rome
Sydney
Cambridge
Edinburgh*
Tarragona*
Los Angeles*
Oxford*

Occupations
racing driver
bus driver
businessman
doctor
teacher
actor
nurse
student
lawyer
secretary
housewife
taxi driver*

Numbers
one
two
three
four
five
six
seven
eight
nine
ten
'oh'
nought

Various
help
hello
down here
home
occupation
and
my*
thank you*
on holiday*

1 occupations

Spell the names of occupations with these letters.

Example: IXTA REVRID = taxi driver

1 TOOCRD ....

2 SUB REVRID ....

3 TTESUND ....

4 SIOFHEUWE ....

5 MISSESUBANN ....

6 TECRAYRES ....

7 CATEHER ....

2 am, is, do

Put *am, is* or *do* in the blanks.

1 What .... your name? – I.......... Steve.

2 What .... you do? – I.......... a teacher.

3 Where .... you live? – In Rome.

4 What .... your name? – I.......... Lucy.

5 Where .... you live? – In New York.

3 what, where

Put *what* or *where* in the blanks.

1 .... do you live? – In London.

2 .... do you do? – I am a student.

3 .... do you live? – In New York.

4 .... is your name? – I am Peter.

5 .... do you do? – I am a businessman.

4 questions

Complete the dialogue.

A: ....

B: Hello.

A: ....?

B: I'm Peter Hedley.

A: Oh . . . .?

B: I'm an actor.

A: ....?

B: In London.

5 read and write

Hello! My name is Hugh Rodgers. I live in Edinburgh and I am a taxi driver. What about you? What do you do? Where do you live?

Now write a similar paragraph about you.

....

....

....

....

2 Classwork

Interaction

1 :

Read the text and fill in Julio's family tree.

Hello! My name is Julio. I am married to a lovely lady called Teresa. We have two sons (Vasco and Carlos) and a daughter, Maria. My father, Francisco, is retired and my mother, Rosa, is a dentist. My brother, Rodrigo, is in France now and my sister, Clara, is at home with my parents.

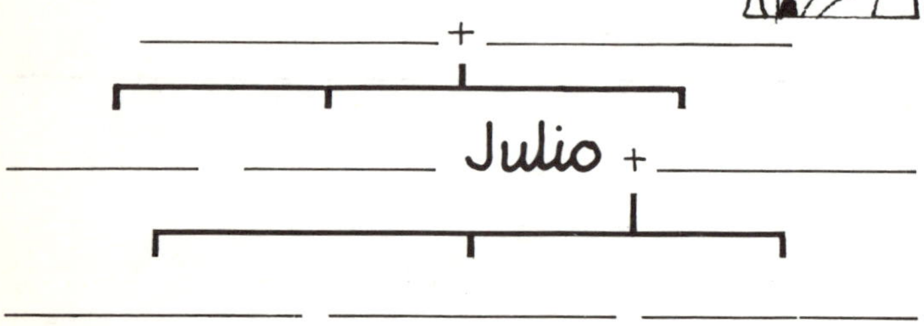

2 : :

Draw family trees about each other's families.
A tells **B**, **C** and **D** about her family. **B**, **C** and **D** draw the family tree and write in the names of the professions of **A**'s family. The group makes family trees for **B**, **C** and **D** in the same way.

3 :

Student **A**: Look at number 1 on page 75. Complete the chart by asking **B** questions.
Student **B**: Look at number 1 on page 81. Complete the chart by asking **A** questions.
Do not look at each other's charts until you have finished.

Listening and acting out

1

Who is the girl in the picture? (Charlotte or Jane?)

2

Write *Jane, her mother* and *her father* under the correct pictures.

....

3

Have conversations like the one on the cassette.

Ask if someone is there.
Ask where they are.

Language summary

New language items

Is your [brother] a [doctor]?
– Yes, he is./No, he isn't.
(= is not)

What does your [brother] do?
– He's a [student].
(= He is)

Where does he live?
– In [London].

Where's [Peter]?
(= Where is)
– He's at [work].
(= He is)

Is Fumiko there?

please OK
thank you goodbye

New vocabulary/expressions * Activity Book vocabulary

Family	*Various*	
mother	good afternoon	we*
father	are	have*
sister	I think	retired*
brother	now	France*
daughter	there	parents*
son	your	boyfriend*
wife	family tree*	engineer*
husband	married*	with*
	lovely*	me*
Places	lady*	
work	called*	
school		

I am	I live
you are	you live
he } is	he } lives
she } is	she } lives
it } is	it } lives
we are	we live
you are	you live
they are	they live

What	do I / do you / does {he, she, it} / do we / do you / do they	do?
Where		live?

1 numbers

Match the telephone numbers and words. The first one is done for you.

a 3-3-7-6	**1** two-nine-eight-seven	**a**	11
b 5-9-2-8	**2** nine-oh-five-six	**b**	....
c 1-4-9-0	**3** two-four-two-five	**c**	....
d 3-3-6-7	**4** two-eight-six-five	**d**	....
e 1-0-9-2	**5** one-four-nine-oh	**e**	....
f 2-9-8-7	**6** six-two-three-oh	**f**	....
g 2-8-6-5	**7** five-nine-two-eight	**g**	....
h 9-0-5-6	**8** one-oh-nine-two	**h**	....
i 6-2-3-0	**9** three-two-oh-seven	**i**	....
j 3-2-0-7	**10** three-three-six-seven	**j**	....
k 2-4-2-5	**11** three-three-seven-six	**k**	....

2

2 am, is, are

Put *am, is* or *are* in the blanks.

1 I .... a student.

2 My brother .... at home.

3 .... your father at work? – Yes, he ....

4 My sister and brother .... at school.

5 .... you a student? – Yes, I ....

3 do, does

Put *do* or *does* in the blanks.

1 What .... you do? – I'm a student.

2 What .... your father do? – He's a doctor.

3 Where .... your brother live? – In Sydney.

4 Where .... you live? – In Manchester.

5 Where .... your two sisters live? – In London.

4 questions

Look at the picture and complete the dialogue.

A: .... your brother?

B: Yes, he is.

A: .... a doctor?

B: No, he isn't.

A: ....?

B: He's a dentist.

A: ....?

B: In Oxford.

A: ....?

B: He's at work.

5 read and write

Read this:

I am Carmen and I am a student. I am at home now. My mother is at work and my brother is at school. My boyfriend, Miguel, is an engineer. He is at home with me now.

Now write a similar paragraph about you.

....

....

....

....

....

....

....

....

....

3 Classwork

Interaction

1

Look at the symbols before playing the game. Listen to the teacher. Put a cross on the correct square when you hear the words. Shout *Bingo*! when all your squares are full.

Symbols:

hospital · helicopter · restaurant · house
post office · airport · pencil · ruler

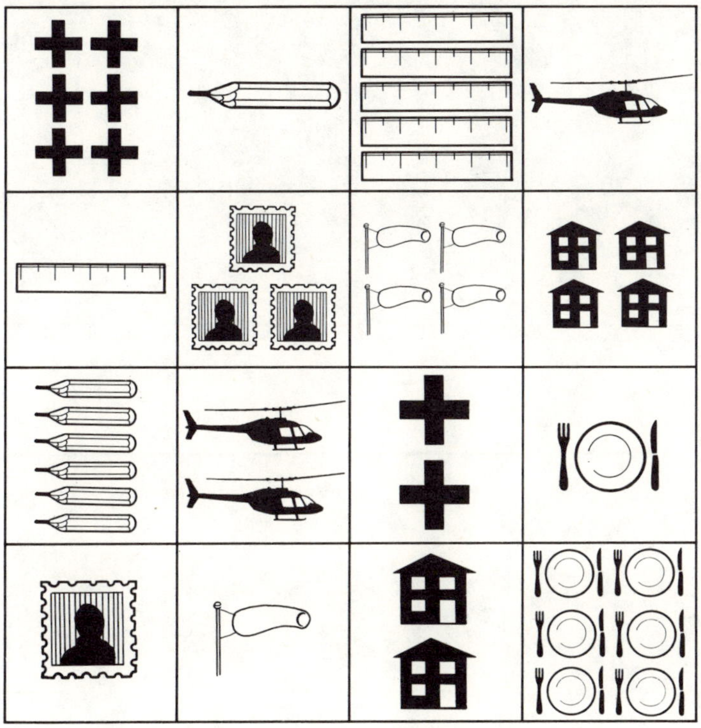

2

Student **A**: Look at number 2 on page 75 and complete the task by asking **B** questions.
Student **B**: Look at number 2 on page 81 and complete the task by asking **A** questions.
Do not look at each other's maps until you have finished.

Listening and acting out

1

Say whether the statements are true or false.

1 Her father is a doctor.
2 Her mother is a doctor.
3 The man is a policeman.

2

Look at the map. Put a cross for the hospital.

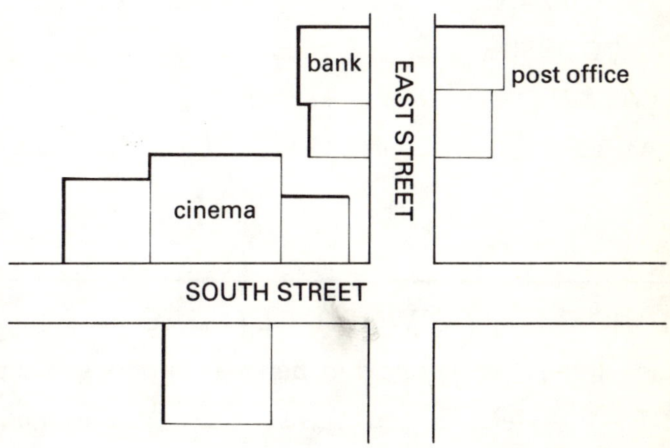

3

Student **A** is at home. His father/mother/sister etc. are not at home. Student **B** is doing a survey and arrives at **A**'s home. Student **B** asks about **A**'s father/mother, etc., and their jobs. Where are they now?

3 Study section

Language summary

New language items

Where's the [post office]?

– It's in [Green Street] { opposite the [bank]. / next to the [cinema]. / between the [bank] and the [cinema].

Excuse me!
– Don't mention it.

Can I have the [glue]?
– Of course. Here you are.
Thanks.

New vocabulary/expressions * Activity Book vocabulary

Places	*Prepositions*	*Various*
cinema	next to	woman
theatre	between	man
station	opposite	drama
restaurant	on	I'm sorry
bank	near	I don't know
post office		house
bus station	*Stationery*	Hey!
street	sellotape	box*
house	glue	shelf
road	ruler	their
airport*	pen	policeman*
hospital*	pencil	central*
	scissors	table
		travel agent*
		travel agency*
		office*
		too*

1 places

Spell names of places with these letters.

Example: NATOTIS = station

1 KANB ....

2 STOPFFIEOC ....

3 TESTURAANR ....

4 NATOTISSUB ....

5 CAIEMN ....

6 ATIRORP ....

2 next, to, between, opposite

Look at the map. Put *next to, between* or *opposite* in the blanks.

1 The hospital is .... the cinema.

2 The bank is .... the cinema.

3 The cinema is .... the bank and the restaurant.

4 The post office is .... the theatre.

5 The post office is .... the bus station.

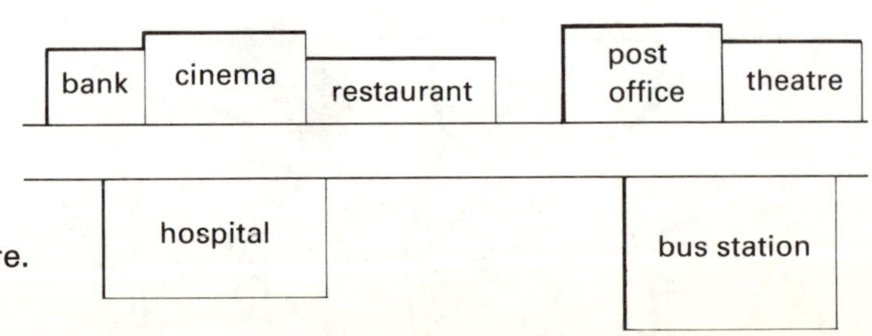

3 am (not), are (not), is (not)

Put *am, is* or *are* in the blanks, with or without *not*.

1 Are you a businessman? – No, I ....

2 My mother .... a nurse at the Central Hospital.

3 Is your father a teacher? – No, he .... He is a bus driver.

4 Is the cinema opposite the hospital? – Yes, it ....

5 The cinema .... next to the hospital, it is opposite it.

4 location of objects

Look at the picture and complete the dialogue.

A: Can I have the scissors?

B: Yes, of course. [1] ....?

A: [2] .... the table.

B: Here you are.

A: Thanks. Can I have the glue?

B: Yes. Where [3] ....?

A: [4] .... the box.

B: Here [5] ....

A: Thanks.

5 read and write

John Richard is a travel agent. He is at work now. His travel agency is in Bridge Street between the post office and the bank. Maggie Shore is a secretary. Her office is in Bridge Street too. It is next to the River Restaurant.

Write a similar text about someone you know. Write what they do, where their office/home is, and where they are now.

....

....

....

....

....

....

....

....

....

....

Interaction

1

Team **A**: use this symbol, **O**
Team **B**: use this symbol, **X**
(*Note*: these symbols are called *noughts* and *crosses*.)

1. Choose a square.
2. Make a sentence or a question with the word in the square.
3. Put your team's symbol in the square for a correct response.
4. The first team with a straight line of **O**s or **X**s wins.

can	is	what
where	what	are
is	are	where

how	where	what
is	are	is
can	what	where

2

Fill in the diagram about someone else in the group and their family.

Father
name
age
nationality
home
occupation

Mother
name
age
nationality
home
occupation

....

Brother
name
age
nationality
home
occupation

Sister
name
age
nationality
home
occupation

Listening and acting out

Ray, Patty, Mike and Sam are at a party.

1

Listen to the cassette and put the sentences in the correct order. (Put the numbers 1, 2, or 3 in the boxes.)

RAY: Mike, this is Patty. ☐
RAY: Hello. I'm Ray. ☐
PATTY: Sam, let me introduce Ray and Mike. ☐

2

Listen to the cassette again. Say whether the statements are true or false.

1. Ray is English T F
2. Patty is Australian. T F
3. Patty lives in Paris. T F
4. Patty is a designer. T F
5. Patty is twenty-five years old. T F

3

You are at a party and you do not know anybody.
You can talk about: name
home
occupation
nationality
age

Language summary

New language items

Where's [Pedro] from?
– He's from [Mexico].
He's [Mexican].
Where are you from?
– I'm from [England].
I'm [English].

Are you English?
– Yes, I am./No, I'm not.

How old { is Carmen? / are you?
– She's / I'm } nineteen.

I'm [Marie] and this is [Jean-Paul].
– Pleased to meet you./Hi.

That's a secret!
(= That is)

New vocabulary/expressions * Activity Book vocabulary

Personal details
age
nationality

Countries
Australia
Spain
Mexico
Germany
France
Italy
Portugal
Greece*
Japan
England

Nationalities
Spanish
Mexican
German
French
Italian
Portuguese
Greek*
Japanese
Irish*

Numbers
eleven
twelve
thirteen
fourteen
fifteen
sixteen
seventeen
eighteen
nineteen
twenty
thirty
forty
fifty
sixty
seventy
eighty
ninety
a hundred

Various
but
welcome
to
how old
party*
designer*
musician*
dancer*

1 nationalities

Change the countries into nationalities and put them in the correct columns.
The first four are done for you. Check your answers with the correct version on page 88.

Mexico
England
Japan
France
Portugal
Switzerland
Puerto Rico
Spain
Germany
America
Australia
China
Brazil
Saudi Arabia
Peru
Hungary
Denmark
Sweden
Turkey
Italy
Greece
Argentina
Holland
Belgium
Yugoslavia
Ireland

-an	-ish	-ese	irregular
Mexican	English	Japanese	French

2 revision

Match the questions and the answers. The first one is done for you.

1 What's your name?	**a** No, she is not.	**1**	b
2 Where do you live?	**b** Michael.	**2**	....
3 What do you do?	**c** In Green Street next to the church.	**3**	....
4 Where is your house?	**d** I am a musician.	**4**	....
5 What does your sister do?	**e** She is a dancer.	**5**	....
6 Is she at home now?	**f** At work.	**6**	....
7 Where is she?	**g** In Manchester.	**7**	....

3 where are you from?

Fill in the blanks with one word only.

1 Is he from America? – No, he is .... He is Australian.

2 .... is Kate from? – She is from Lisbon. She is Portuguese.

3 Gerry and Bernadette are not from England. They .... Irish.

4 Marie is from Switzerland. She is ....

5 Is Raul .... Colombia? – No he is not. He is Bolivian.

4 where, what, how old

Put *where, what* or *how old* in the blanks.

1 .... is Monica from? – She is English.

2 .... does she live? – In Singapore.

3 .... does she do? – She is a student.

4 .... is she? – Twenty.

5 .... is her house? – Opposite the First National Bank.

5 conversation

You meet Pete and Mary at a cocktail party. Write what you say.

PETE: Hello.

YOU: 1 ....

PETE: I'm Pete and this is Mary.

YOU: 2 ....

PETE: What's your name?

YOU: 3 ....

PETE: And where are you from?

YOU: 4 ....

PETE: Really! What do you do?

YOU: 5 ....

PETE: We're teachers. And where do you live?

YOU: 6 ....

5 Classwork

Interaction

1

Look at the pictures. Put the words below in the right speech bubbles.

Kostas. | Where's he from? | Where were you yesterday evening? | He's a pilot. | Greece.

2

Choose someone in the class and complete this chart about them.

NAME: .... *AGE:* ....

HOME: ....

OCCUPATION: ....

NATIONALITY: ....

MOVEMENTS:

1 ten o'clock yesterday morning

....

2 three o'clock yesterday afternoon

....

3 five o'clock yesterday afternoon

....

4 nine o'clock yesterday evening

....

Listening and acting out

1

Listen to the cassette and answer the questions.

1 The inspector thinks:
- **a** Charlie's a policeman.
- **b** Charlie's a thief.
- **c** Charlie's a doctor.

2 Where was Charlie:
- **a** at nine o'clock?
- **b** at ten o'clock?

3 Who was Charlie with at ten o'clock?

2

Look. This was the bank at 10 o'clock last night.

Student **A** is a policeman. Ask the others about last night. Were they the thieves?

Language summary

New language items

Were you [at home] [yesterday evening]?
– Yes, I was./No, I wasn't.
(= was not)

Where were you on Monday afternoon?
– I was at [the bank].

What's the time?
(= What is)
– It's ten o'clock.
(= It is)

Fumiko speaking.
– I forgot. I'm sorry.

I was
you were
she }
he } was
it }
we were
you were
they were

New vocabulary/expressions * Activity Book vocabulary

Past time expressions
yesterday morning
yesterday afternoon
yesterday evening

Days of the week
Monday
Tuesday
Wednesday
Thursday
Friday
Saturday
Sunday

Places
disco
hotel
supermarket
cafeteria*

Various
come in
these
for
alone
who
with
pilot
back
tour guide
think*
thief*
girlfriend*
until*
Canadian*
last*
night*

1 places

Find the six names of places and put a line round them. One is done for you.

C	A	D	I	S	C	O	B	C	D	S	E
F	D	G	H	I	F	J	K	M	M	O	N
O	P	E	Q	R	G	S	T	N	V	P	W
S	U	P	E	R	M	A	R	K	E	T	Q
X	A	Z	K	Y	H	C	I	N	E	M	A
E	F	N	G	K	J	H	H	L	N	Q	K
M	A	Z	S	T	A	T	I	O	N	R	R
B	A	E	T	I	L	K	O	G	T	M	U
T	X	P	W	L	N	N	Z	V	M	E	Q
H	O	S	P	I	T	A	L	O	Y	J	L

2 time

Write the time in the spaces. The first one is done for you.

1  *It is 3 o'clock.* ....

2  ....

3  ....

4  ....

5  ....

6  ....

7  ....

8  ....

9  ....

10  ....

3 word order

Put the words and phrases in order to make correct sentences.

Example: [in London] [yesterday.] [I was]

I was in London yesterday.

1 [at home] [at seven o'clock] [yesterday.] [I was]

....

2 [in Paris.] [a doctor] [and] [she lives] [Jane Green] [is]

....

3 [at home,] [Mark] [he is] [is not] [at school.]

....

4 [from?] [Canadian.] [is] [Where is] [She] [Joan]

....

5 [do] [do?] [you] [What] [an engineer.] [I am]

....

4 was, were

Put *was* or *were* in the blanks (with or without *not*).

1 .... you at the cinema yesterday evening? – No, I ....

2 Yesterday morning Mr Jones .... at the bank.

3 Yesterday evening Philip and Susan .... at the disco.

4 At seven o'clock Mr and Mrs Scofield .... at the theatre, they were at the cinema.

5 Yesterday afternoon I .... at home with my mother.

5 read and write

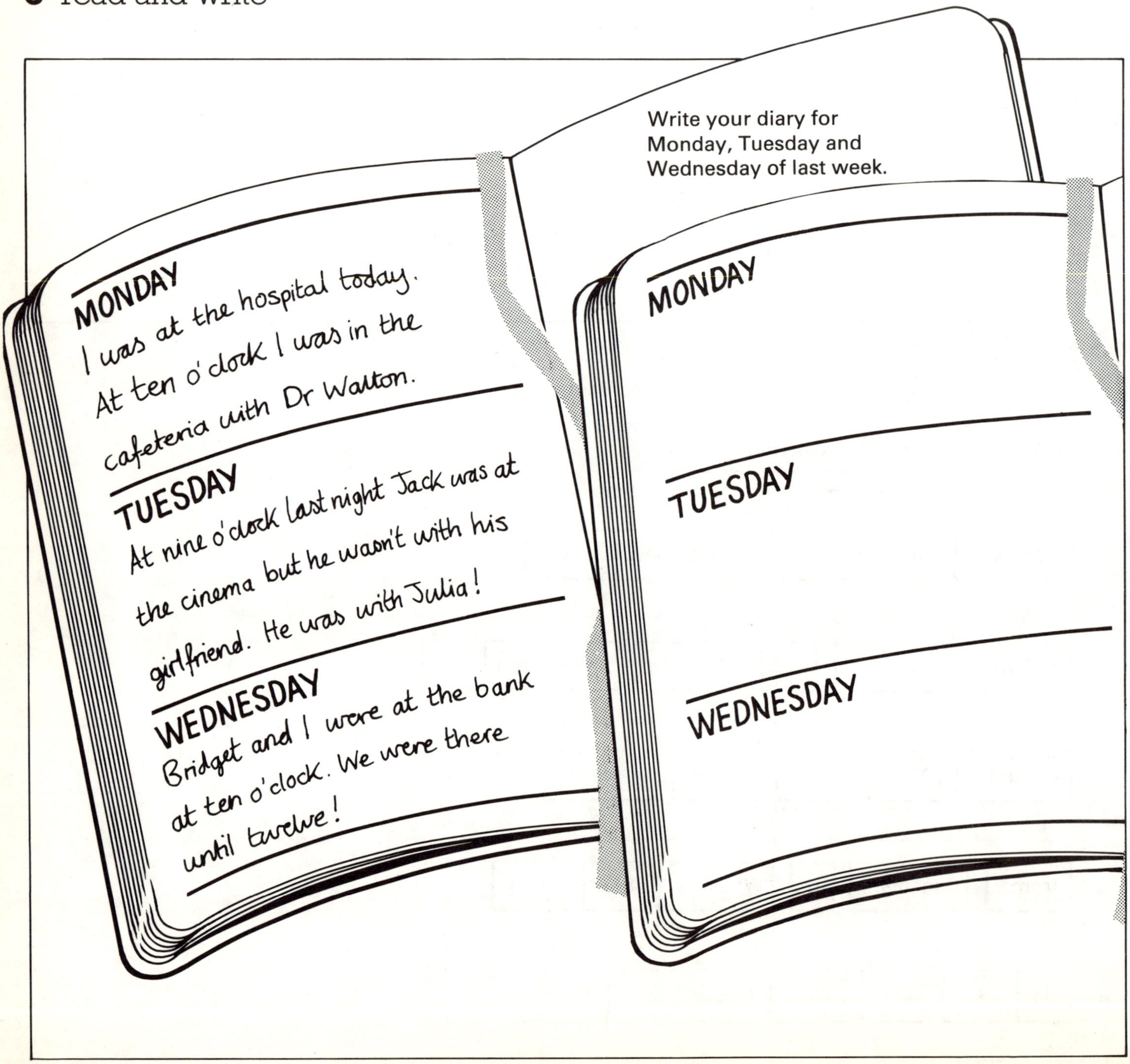

6 Classwork

Interaction

1

Decide which clothes are Jane's and which are Kate's. Ask *Whose skirt is this?* etc.

2

Look at the symbols before you play the game. Listen to the teacher. Put a cross on the correct square when you hear the words. Shout *Bingo!* when all the squares are full.

Symbols: scissors lighter ruler this pen sellotape that

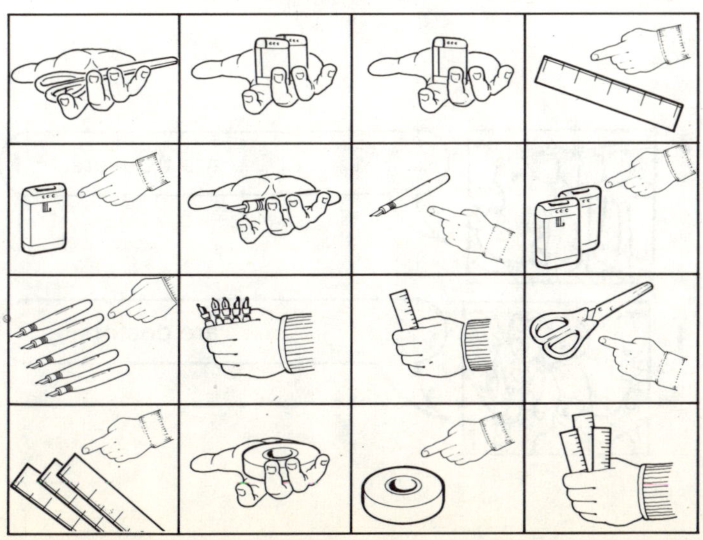

Listening and acting out

1

Listen to the cassette and answer the questions.

1. Where are George and Judith?
2. Whose hat is it?
3. Whose coat is it?
4. Whose party is it?

2

Choose the correct answers.

1 What time is it?
a ten o'clock
b eleven o'clock
c twelve o'clock

2 Where were the gloves?

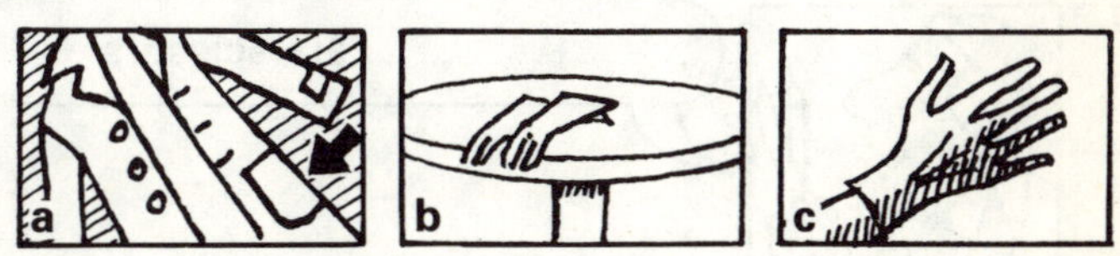

3

At the end of a party you go home.
Talk about the time.
Get your hats, coats and gloves.
Say goodbye and thank you.

6 Study section

Language summary

New language items

Whose sweater is { this? / that? }
– It's [John's].
(= It is)

Whose shoes are { these? / those? }
– They're { mine. / yours. / his. / hers. }

Is this yours?

Can I borrow { it? / them? }

. . . I think

New vocabulary/expressions * Activity Book vocabulary

Clothes
skirt
sweater
jacket
shirt
trousers
shoes
boots
gloves
hat*
coat*
dress*

Personal articles
book
glasses
lighter
matches

Various
passenger
to come
this way
here we go
today
tomorrow
everybody
camera
equipment
mine
cameraman
television
reporter
don't
again
sir
present (home)
photograph*
police station*
(bus) depot*
waiter*

1 clothes

Fill in the letters to make the names of clothes. Circle *his* and/or *hers*. This depends on whether they are for a man or a woman.

Example: T <u>I</u> <u>E</u> (his) /hers

1 G — — — S — —	his/hers		**5** T — — — S — — —	his/hers
2 D — E — —	his/hers		**6** S — — — T — —	his/hers
3 B — — — S	his/hers		**7** J — — — E —	his/hers
4 S — O — —	his/hers		**8** S — — R —	his/hers

2 this, that, these, those

Put *this, that, these* or *those* in the blanks.

1 

.... are scissors.

2 

.... is the post office

3 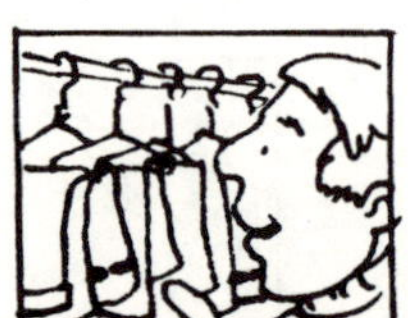

.... are trousers.

4 

.... are doctors.

5  .... is my tie.

6  .... is my home.

7 

.... is my bank.

8  .... are pens.

3 mine, his, hers, ours, theirs and whose

Complete the questions and answers.
(*his, hers, theirs, mine*)

= mine = his = hers = theirs

Example: Whose pen is this? – It is his.

1 .... house is that? – It is ....

2 Whose gloves .... these? – They are ....

3 .... pencil .... this? – It is ....

4 .... matches .... these? – They are ....

5 Whose lighter is this? ....

4 general revision

In the following sentences choose the correct alternative, **a** or **b**.

Example: I **a** were / **b** was in London. b

1 John **a** lives / **b** live in London. ....

2 Mark is not **a** in / **b** at home, he is at school. ....

3 Where **a** John's house is? / **b** is John's house? ....

4 What **a** do / **b** does you do? ....

5 John is from **a** English; / **b** England; Mary is from France. ....

5 read and write

This is my sister. Her name is Mary. She is a bus driver and she lives in London. That is her house in the photograph. Mary's bus depot is in Kennington Road, but she lives in William Road, next to the police station. Mary's husband is Italian and he is a waiter. His name is Nino. Mary is with Nino in this photograph.

Stick a photograph of someone in your family in the space. Write a paragraph (like the one about Mary) about the person in your photograph.

7 Classwork

Interaction

1:

a In pairs put the sentences in the correct order to make a dialogue. Number the sentences. The first sentence is already numbered for you.

1 Good morning. Can I help you?

When do you want your appointment?

Goodbye.

Ten o'clock? Yes. Thank you very much.

Good morning. I want an appointment with Doctor Fowler.

Yes, that's OK. Can you come at ten o'clock?

On Thursday the 9th, if that's all right.

2:

a Find out the meaning of these words. (Ask your teacher or use a dictionary.)

sitting room, dining room, bathroom, kitchen, studio, bedroom, guest room.

b Student **A**: Look at number 3 on page 76. Put the names in the correct rooms by asking **B**.
Student **B**: Look at number 3 on page 82. Put the names in the correct rooms by asking **A**.
Do not look at each other's plans until you have finished.

Listening and acting out

1

Listen to the cassette and answer the questions.

1 Where does Miss Shore want to go?
2 Does she want first class or tourist class?
3 Who is the extra seat for?

2

Listen to the cassette again and complete the chart.

NAME:	
ADDRESS:	
FLIGHT TO	*DATE*
1	....
2	....
3	....
4	....

Student **A** is a travel agent
Student **B** rings up to book a flight

Talk about:
Where? (Madrid, New York, etc.)
When? (27th February, 4th March, etc.)
What class? (first class/tourist class)

Language summary

New language items

When's [your birthday]?
(= When is)
– [4th July].

It's	half	past [six].
	ten quarter	to/past [six].

I want to hire a car.
– Certainly sir. That will be all right.

New vocabulary/expressions * Activity Book vocabulary

Months
January
February
March
April
May
June
July
August
September
October
November
December

Numbers
first
second
third
fourth
fifth
sixth
seventh
eighth
ninth
tenth
twentieth
thirtieth (etc.)

Places
opera house
harbour
factory
hairdresser's
chemist's*
the Eiffel Tower
the Coliseum

Rooms
sitting room*
dining room*
bathroom*
kitchen*
studio*
bedroom*
guest room*

Various
car
newest
next
race
day
manager
problem
birthday
half past
quarter past
date
place
friend
colleague
to hire
to book a table
good morning
room
address
to make an appointment
tonight
ticket
flight*
advertisement
happy
job
travel
airline
world
week*
to help*
patient*
first class*
tourist class*
extra*
seat*
beach*
sailor*
diplomat*
old*
children*
marital status*
single*

1 dates

Match the words and numbers. The first one is done for you.

a	1/1	**1**	the fifth of April	**a**	7
b	5/4	**2**	the seventeenth of March	**b**	....
c	4/7	**3**	the twenty-seventh of April	**c**	....
d	17/3	**4**	the thirty-first of August	**d**	....
e	22/10	**5**	the eleventh of February	**e**	....
f	31/8	**6**	the fourth of July	**f**	....
g	11/2	**7**	the first of January	**g**	....
h	27/4	**8**	the twenty-second of October	**h**	....

2 time

Write the time in the spaces provided. The first one is done for you.

1  It is half past nine.

2  ....

3  ....

4  ....

5  ....

6  ....

3 punctuation: capitals

Put a circle round the words that should start with a capital letter.

Example: (june) businessman (moscow) (We write *June* and *Moscow*.)

john teacher chemist's holland beach gloves bank mother

son spanish jacket trousers home jane anna pilot ankara

paris january agatha christie sailor supermarket

4 what, when, where, whose

Put *what, when, where* or *whose* in the blanks.

1 .... do you do? – I am a student.

2 .... were you yesterday afternoon? – At the restaurant.

3 .... is your house? – In Newmarket Road opposite the school.

4 .... is your birthday? – 24th January.

5 .... do you live? – In Cambridge.

6 .... house is this? – It is mine.

7 .... are you from? – I am Turkish.

8 .... is your sister? – She is at work.

5 read and write

Julio Branco is a Portuguese diplomat from Lisbon. Julio is fifty-six years old and his birthday is on 10th August. Julio was in Brazil from 1975–1982. Now he lives in Vila Franca with his wife, Teresa, and their three children.

Write a similar paragraph about Tom King.

Name: Tom King
Nationality: Australian (Sydney)
Parents' home: Sydney
Age: 36
Birthday: 15/9
Visit: England, 1980–1984
Present home: Cedar Road, Sydney
Marital status: single

....

....

....

....

....

....

....

....

....

Now write a similar text about someone from your country.

8 Classwork

Interaction

1 :

Complete this paragraph with information about another student.

(Name) ____________ is ____________ years old. She/he is from ____________ and she/he lives in ____________. Her/his birthday is on ____________. When she/he was ten years old her/his favourite food was ____________ and her/his favourite song was ____________. ____________ likes music, and she/he likes ____________ best, but she/he does not like ____________.

2 : :

a Fill in the subject column in the survey form with the names of famous sportsmen, singers, actors, etc.

b Ask people if they like the personalities in your survey. Record their answers with a tick (√) for yes, a cross (×) for no, and a question mark (?) 'don't know'.

Subject	*yes*	*no*	*don't know*

Listening and acting out

1

Listen to the cassette and answer the questions.

1 What does Bart Scott do?
2 Where is Bart Scott from?
3 Where does he live now?

2

Listen to the cassette again and say whether the statements are true or false.

1 Bart does not like India. T F
2 Bart likes curry. T F
3 Bart likes New York best. T F
4 Bart likes his own music best. T F

3

Student **A** is a famous 'celebrity', student **B** is an interviewer on a television programme. **B** asks **A** about his home, nationality, likes and dislikes, etc.

8 Study section

Language summary

New language items

Do you like [steak]?
– Yes, I do./No, I don't.
(= do not)
– I don't know, I've never tried it.
(= I have)

What's [spaghetti bolognese]?
– It's an [Italian] dish with [pasta] and [minced meat].

What's your favourite sport?
(= What is)

I like [running] best.
– I like [running] too.
– I don't.

I like	do I like?
you like	do you like?
he likes	does he like?
she likes	does she like?
it likes	does it like?
we like	do we like?
you like	do you like?
they like	do they like?

New vocabulary/expressions * Activity Book vocabulary

Food
food
octopus
spaghetti
paella
raw fish
steak
shepherd's pie
moussaka
spaghetti bolognese
ratatouille
roast beef
potatoes
minced meat
aubergines
cheese
pasta
onions
mole
courgettes
tomatoes
sauce
chocolate
chilli
curry
houmous*
rice*
chicken*
seafood*

Sports
sport
football
tennis
bull-fighting
running
swimming
boxing
skiing
rowing*

Various
survey
could
answer
some
question
well
good
ugh!
look!
must
to go
to wait
to love
to hate
dish
singer
Taurus
sun
fast
favourite
our
to see
song*
famous*
music*
subject*
India*
steward*
dancing*
films*
likes*
dislikes*
how boring*
both*
on holiday*
country*
fantastic*

1 sport

Write the name of the sport by the picture. One is done for you.

1 

rowing

2 

3 

4 

5 

6 

7 

8 

2 do, does

Write *do* or *does* in the blanks.

1 Where .... you live? – in Paris.

2 What .... John do? – He's a teacher.

3 Where .... your mother and father live? – In London.

4 .... Peter like raw fish? – No, he does not.

5 My friends John and Mary .... not like paella.

6 .... you like paella? – Yes, I love it.

3 punctuation: capitals

Put a circle round words that should start with a capital letter.

Example: (tom) is an actor. (he) lives in (sydney). (We write *Tom, Sydney* and *He.*) *He* has a capital letter here because it is the first word in the sentence.

christopher williams is a steward for an airline. he is married to sharon. she is a pilot and they live in uxbridge.

last night christopher and sharon were at the disco. sharon likes dancing, but christopher does not. he likes films best.

4 conversation: likes/dislikes (food)

Complete the dialogue.

1 Have some houmous.

2 No thank you! I .... like it!

3 Do you like moussaka?

4 What is it?

5 It's a (Greek, aubergines, cheese, minced meat) ....

.... Do you want some?

6 No, thank you.

7 What's your favourite food, then?

8 Well, I think I like shepherd's pie ....

9 Oh, how boring! Don't you like any Greek food?

10 I don't know. I've .... tried it.

11 Well then! Now's the time! Waiter!

5 read and write

Carol in Spain

Carol's Cooking Page

In February and March last year I was on holiday. From 24th February to 6th March, I was in France, and from 6th March to 18th March, I was in Spain.

The food in both countries was fantastic, but I like paella best! It is a Spanish dish with rice, chicken and seafood. I had paella when I was in Valencia.

Carol has visited your country. Write 'Carol's cooking page' after her visit.

Carol's Cooking Page

Carol in ....

9 Classwork

Interaction

1

Ask other students questions to complete the chart.

Find someone who:

a plays a musical instrument ....

b was at a restaurant last night ....

c reads a newspaper after breakfast ....

d likes rock music ....

e goes jogging ....

2

Student **A**: Look at number 4 on page 76. Complete the chart by asking **B** and **C**.
Student **B**: Look at number 4 on page 82. Complete the chart by asking **A** and **C**.
Student **C**: Look at number 4 on page 87. Complete the chart by asking **A** and **B**.

Do not look at each other's charts until you have finished.

What time does flight 389 leave?

Where does flight 951 go?

Which is the gate for the flight to Paris?

What time does flight 006 arrive?

3

Complete the blanks with information from the flight timetable.

1 A: Which is the gate for the flight to Mexico City?

B: .... It leaves at ....

A: Help! That's in five minutes!

2 A: Stewardess! What number is this flight?

B: 027.

A: Where ....?

B: ....

A: Oh no! I want flight .... to Paris.

Listening and acting out

1

Listen to the cassette and fill in the chart.

NAME: Angela Stansgate

SYMPTOMS:
Where is the pain?

stomach	☐
chest	☐
head	☐
legs	☐

HABITS:
Does the patient

	yes	no
smoke?	☐	☐
take exercise?	☐	☐

2

Listen to the cassette again and write down the doctor's recommendations.

DOCTOR'S RECOMMENDATIONS

1 ______________________

2 ______________________

3 ______________________

3

Have similar conversations. Student **A** is the doctor, student **B** is the patient. The doctor should ask the patient about the pain and his/her habits. The doctor should make recommendations.

9 Study section

Language summary

New language items

What time do you [have breakfast]?
– At [half past seven].

How do you go to [work]?
– By [car]./On foot.

What do you do [in the evening]?
– I usually [listen to music].

How much is a return ticket to [King's Lynn]?

Which is the platform for [King's Lynn]?

That's in [four] minutes.

I get up
you get up
he/she/it gets up
we get up
you get up
they get up

What time do I get up?
What time do you get up?
What time does { he get up? / she get up? / it get up? }
What time do we get up?
What time do you get up?
What time do they get up?

New vocabulary/expressions * Activity Book vocabulary

Everyday activities
to wake up
to have { breakfast / lunch / dinner }
to leave home
to get { home / to work }
to get up
to go to bed
to drive*

Leisure
to watch
to listen to
to read
to play
darts
jogging
swimming
chess
musical instrument*
to smoke*
to take exercise*
cards*

Travel
on foot
train
bike
destination
single
return
pound
platform
number
minute
to arrive
price
gate*
stewardess*

Various
to tell
went
usually
canteen
at the weekend
on Mondays
in the evening
cornflakes
institute
Indian

to open
newspaper*
stomach*
chest*
head*
legs*
pain*
bath*
the movies*
Hong Kong*
every*
ambulance*
garage*
private*
language*
class*
everyday*
Kuwait*
Indonesia*
to start*
optional*
principal*
Canada*
United States of America*
previous*
businesswoman*

1 everyday and leisure activities

Match the following verbs and phrases. The first one is done for you.

1 read	**a** at 6 o'clock	**1** h
2 watch	**b** cards	**2** ....
3 go to	**c** music	**3** ....
4 listen to	**d** home	**4** ....
5 play	**e** a bath	**5** ....
6 arrive	**f** swimming	**6** ....
7 get up	**g** the movies	**7** ....
8 go	**h** a newspaper	**8** ....
9 have	**i** by bus	**9** ....
10 travel	**j** television	**10** ....

2 word order

Put the words and phrases in order to make correct sentences.

Example: [in Hong Kong] [yesterday.] [I was]

I was in Hong Kong yesterday.

1 [is] [the hotel] [The Dominion Theatre] [next to] [in Granton Road.]

....

2 [is] [Peter's] [July.] [21st] [birthday] [on]

....

3 [every morning.] [gets up] [Mary] [at five o'clock]

....

4 [with] [a Spanish dish] [is] [chicken and seafood.] [Paella]

....

5 [on Sundays.] [John] [plays tennis] [usually]

....

3 present simple: verb endings

Write the correct form of the verb in brackets.

Example: Peter usually (*go*) ....goes.... jogging in the mornings.

1 Peter is an ambulance driver. He (*get*) .... up at six o'clock.

2 Peter's two sisters, Mary and Emma, (*leave*) .... home at half past seven.

3 Mary and Emma (*get*) .... to school at quarter to nine.

4 Peter (*have*) .... lunch at one o'clock.

5 Emma and Mary (*have*) .... lunch at half past one.

6 Peter (*read*) .... a newspaper in the evenings.

7 Mary and Emma (*go*) .... to bed at eleven o'clock.

4 comprehension and revision

Read the passage and fill in the blanks with one word only.

Peter is twenty-three years[1] .... and he lives in Birmingham with [2].................... mother and father.

Every day Peter gets up [3].................... six o'clock and he goes jogging. Then he has [4].................... and drives to work. [5].................... gets to the hospital at eight o'clock.

Yesterday Peter's car [6].................... in the garage.

Peter was not at work at eight o'clock, he was on a bus!

[7].................... favourite sport is football but he [8].................... skiing too. He usually plays tennis at weekends.

5 read and write

The Mill Language School

Until 1932 The Mill was a private hospital but now it is a language school for students from Italy to Indonesia, from Kuwait to Brazil. Every day students get to the school at quarter to nine. Classes start at nine o'clock and lunch is at one. In the afternoon students go to 'optional' classes. In the evening they eat at the school restaurant or watch television in the student TV room.

The principal of the school is Roger Arnold. Roger was a singer but now he teaches English.

Write a similar text about the Mersey Music School.

Name: Mersey Music School

Students: from England, Canada and the United States of America.

Daily activities: Classes 8.30–12.30 Lunch 12.45
Drama classes in the afternoon
Evening: read newspapers, play darts/chess

Principal: Angela Naseby, music teacher

Previous job: Businesswoman

....
....
....
....
....
....
....
....
....
....
....
....

Write about a school you know in the same way.

10 Classwork

Interaction

1 ●●● ●●●

Read these instructions:

1 Write a different word in each space below.
2 Divide into two teams.
3 A member from team **A** chooses a number from 1–16.
4 A member of team **B** says his/her word for that number.
5 The member of team **A** uses that word in a sentence or question. He or she gets a point if the sentence or question is correct.

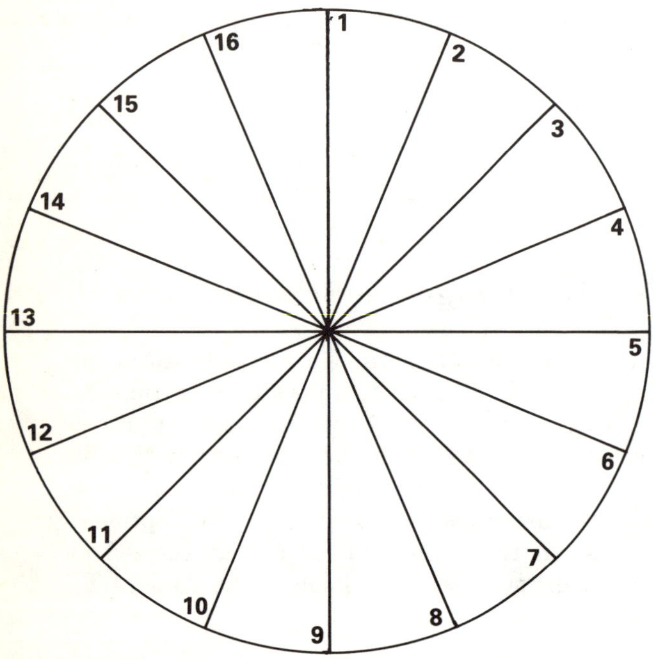

2 ●●

Student **A**: Look at number 5 on page 77. Find the similarities between your picture and **B**'s by asking **B**.
Student **B**: Look at number 5 on page 83. Find the similarities between your picture and **A**'s by asking **A**.
Do not look at each other's pictures until you have finished.

Listening and acting out

1

Match George Hayes, Fenella Orchard, Stella Richards and Albert Winterton with their ideal husband or wife.

a	a short man with glasses and a beard	b	a tall thin woman with blue eyes and blond hair
c	a tall thin man with grey hair and blue eyes	d	a short woman with brown eyes and a happy face

2

Have similar conversations. Student **A** works at *Find Your Partner* and student **B** wants a husband/wife. Student **A** asks **B** about the 'ideal' husband/wife.

Ask: short/tall?
how old?
colour of eyes?

Language summary

New language items

What colour is [Jane's hair]?
– It's [grey].

What colour are [Jane's eyes]?
– They're [brown].

What does [Peter] look like?
– He's a [fat man] with [brown hair].

Can I help you?

One / A pair { of those } sweaters. / shoes.

Which colour?

What size?

New vocabulary/expressions * Activity Book vocabulary

Colours
colour
blue
brown
green
grey
black
white
fair
blond
pink*

Description
to describe
good-looking
short
tall
thin
fat
young
middle-aged
new
hair
eyes
horrible
girl
boy
height
size
small
medium
large
intelligent*
stupid*
big*
strong*
weak*
pretty*
handsome*
ugly*
kind*
unkind*
sad*

Various
to help
officer
lost
spot
ill
dog
new
tie
earrings
travel
programme
article
employed
tea
coffee
sandwiches
beard*
to find*
partner*
dinner*
to visit*
to type*
letters*
squash*
drawer*

1 descriptive adjectives

Put the following adjectives in pairs with opposite meanings. The first one is done for you. You may use a dictionary.

tall
intelligent
thin
stupid
small
new
old
fat
kind
old
weak
big
young
pretty
ugly
unkind
happy
handsome
ugly
sad
strong
short

tall, short
....
....
....
....
....
....
....
....
....
....

2 is/are, was/were

Write *is, are, was* or *were* in the blanks.

1 What colour .... John's tie? – It's blue.

2 Mary and Emma .... young girls.

3 Emma's eyes .... green.

4 Mary's hair .... brown.

5 Mrs Smith's hair .... black, but now it .... white.

6 Mary and Emma .... at the cinema yesterday evening.

7 What colour .... John's trousers? – They .... brown.

3 descriptions

Write a sentence of description for each of the following pictures.

1 ....

2 ....

3 ....

4 ....

5 ....

4 revision

In the following sentences choose the correct alternative, **a** or **b**.

Example: I **a** were / **b** was in London. .....b.....

1 Do you like octopus? Yes I **a** do. / **b** like. ....

2 Mary is **a** young girl. / **b** a young girl. ....

3 They **a** has / **b** have dinner at eight o'clock.

4 James is a young man with brown **a** hair. / **b** hairs.

5 **a** This / **b** These are my books. ....

5 punctuation: capitals and full stops

Rewrite this paragraph using capital letters and putting full stops where necessary.

Example: john is a businessman he lives in London

John is a businessman. He lives in London.

alistair is thirty-two years old he is a doctor and he lives in london alistair is a handsome man with blue eyes and black hair last week he was in paris alistair usually visits paris in february

....

....

....

....

6 two word puzzles

A

A Clues

Across **2** Can I have one of those  please? (8)

3 His eyes are ...., not brown or blue. (5)

5 Are .... your glasses? (5) 

7 He's very .... He's only fifteen. (5)

4 Two days after the ninth is the .... (8)

Down **1** She .... plays squash on Sundays. (7)

2 She types letters. She's a .... (9)

6 Nine, ... eleven (3)

B Clues

Across **1** These are  (8)

6 He is number one at the bank. He is the bank .... (7)

7 My favourite sport is .... (6)

9 One box, two .... (5)

Down **2** They were .... the drawer. (2)

3 Now they're .... the table. (2)

4 The cinema is in Green .... (6)

5 I usually .... at seven o'clock in the morning. (4,2)

8 A new pair of . (5)

B

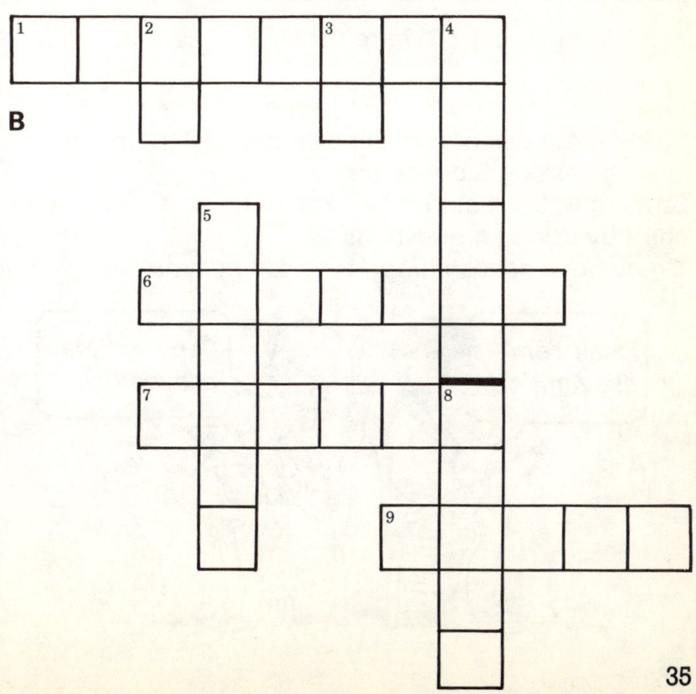

11 Classwork

Interaction

1:

Look at the pictures. Put the words and phrases below in the right speech bubbles.

Thanks very much. | Where can I see a good film? | Yes? | You can try the Arts Cinema. | It's in Park Street opposite the supermarket. | Yes. | Where's that?

2:

Student **A**: Look at number 6 on page 78. Complete the chart by asking **B** questions.
Student **B**: Look at number 6 on page 84. Complete the chart by asking **A** questions.
Do not look at each other's charts until you have finished.

Listening and acting out

1

Listen to the cassette and say whether the statements are true or false.

1 The man works in a theatre.
2 Miss Peabody is a secretary.
3 The man wants a secretary.

2

Listen to the cassette again. Complete this form.

NAME:		
ABILITIES:	**yes**	**no**
Can type?	☐	☐
Can take shorthand?	☐	☐
OTHER ABILITIES		
1		
2		
3		
4		

3

Have job interviews. Student **A** wants a job as a secretary and is interviewed by student **B**. **B** fills in the form based on **A**' abilities.

NAME:	**yes**	**no**
ABILITIES: Can type?	☐	☐
Can take shorthand?	☐	☐
What languages can he/she speak?	☐	☐

Language summary

New language items

Can Antonio type?
– Yes, he can./No he can't.
(= he can not)

Where can I [see a good film]?
– You can try the [Studio Cinema].

You look [tired]. Do you want some help?
– I'll be all right.

I can
you can
he / she / it } can
we can
you can
they can

New vocabulary/expressions * Activity Book vocabulary

Entertainment
concert hall
gallery
classical
exhibition
paintings

Mental and physical states
worried
tired
exhausted
nervous
upset
angry*

Various
taken
to sit down
really
a little
American
that sounds interesting!
to study
to cook
piano
to speak
to hear
to try
to buy
clothes
island
Europe
season
Latin America
hall
garden
boutique
shop
ability
to skate
to ski
swimming pool
guitar
to read music
homework
to look
(to find) keys
to start (a car)
to lift
to remember lines
early
late
to take shorthand
baseball*
beautiful*
paradise*
to eat*
top-class*
king*
excellent*
play*
only*
modern*
shopping centre*
town*

1 vocabulary: mental and physical states

Put the letters in the right order to make the words for mental and physical states.
The first one is done for you.

1 EHSEDAUXT exhausted

2 GRAYN ....

3 ERNVSOU ....

4 DTRIE ....

5 TSEPU ....

6 IRODWRE ....

2 can(not), do/does (not), am/is/are (not)

Put *can*(*not*), *do/does* (*not*) or *am/is/are* (*not*) in the blanks.

1 Can John play the piano? – Yes, he ....
2 Does he play the piano in the evenings? – No, he ....
3 Can he play the guitar? – Yes, he ....
4 Is John tall? – Yes, he ....
5 Does John like Indian food? – Yes, he ....
6 Are you English? – No, I ....
7 Can you speak French? – Yes, I ....
8 Do you play tennis? – Yes, we ....
9 Can you play the guitar? – Yes, I ....

3 can, can't

Look at the chart. Then write five sentences using *can* and *can't* about the information it contains.

			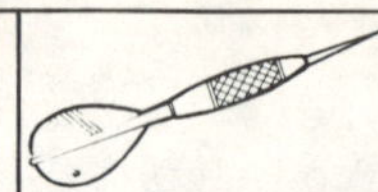	
MARK	✓	✗	✗	✗
KATIE	✗	✓	✗	✓
THE TWINS	✗	✗	✓	✓

1 ....

2 ....

3 ....

4 ....

5 ....

4 read and write

COME TO BEAUTIFUL NORTHBOURNE!
The tourist's paradise!

- you can swim from the beaches
- you can eat at one of our top-class restaurants (for £15 you eat like a king)
- you can see excellent plays at the Majestic theatre or watch a good film at the Royal Cinema for only £3.00
- you can buy beautiful modern clothes at the new Kite Shopping Centre

NORTHBOURNE IS THE TOWN FOR YOU.
COME TODAY.

Write a similar text about Southbourne.

SOUTHBOURNE

- The Rainbow Gallery of Modern Art
- Greek food at the Athens Restaurant (£10 a person)
- The Arts Cinema
- The Midsummer Shopping Centre

Write a similar text about your town.

12 Classwork

Interaction

1 ⁘

Team **A**: use this symbol, **O**
Team **B**: use this symbol, **X**
(*Note*: these symbols are called *noughts* and *crosses.*)

1. Choose a square.
2. Make a sentence with the word in the square.
3. Put your team's symbol in the square for a correct response.
4. The first team with a straight line of **0**s or **X**s wins.

always	can't	tall
his	leaves	mine
like	between	was

can	eyes	first
often	twice	were
opposite	onions	those

2 :

Complete this questionnaire about your partner. Ask your partner how often he or she does the things and write the answers in the chart.

NAME: ....

AGE: ....

OCCUPATION: ....

FREQUENCY OF LEISURE ACTIVITIES

**watch television* ....

**listen to music* ....

**read magazines* ....

**take exercise* ....

**play cards* ....

**play chess* ....

**go to a restaurant/bar* ....

**go to the cinema* ....

Listening and acting out

1

Listen to the cassette and answer the questions.

1. Who is Bud Samson?
2. Where are Terry and Bud?
3. What is Bud's hobby?
4. What is Bud's favourite food?

2

Listen to the cassette again. Put Bud's activities with the correct adverb.

always ....

often ....

usually ....

sometimes ....

3

In groups of three have interviews like the one on the cassette. Student **A** is a famous personality. Students **B** and **C** are reporters. They ask **A** about his/her activities, hobbies, likes and dislikes, etc.

Language summary

New language items

What does [Philip] do on [Saturdays]?
– He [always] gets up before [seven o'clock].

How often do you [play football]?
– About [twice] a [week].

Do you [paint] well?
– Not very well.
– Not too badly.
– Quite well.

Could you [paint] me [a picture]?
– All right.
– I'd rather not.

New vocabulary/expressions * Activity Book vocabulary

Frequency
always
often
sometimes
rarely
once
twice
[three] times

Hobbies
to sing a song
to give (me) a game
to play a tune
to teach (me) to skate
to paint a picture
tennis racket
chess set
trumpet
paints
skates

Various
year
let's
folk club
want to
true
records
to go out
to sit
flat
before
to sleep
all
hobby
dear
to know
to say
life
to fly
across
the Atlantic
route
if
meal
so
ordinary
see you soon
present
speech
dance
coffee bar
record*
club*
manager*
detective*
colleague*
sauna (bath)*
lesson*
sex*
frequency*
leisure*
activity*
magazine*
bar*
stamp*
taxi*
fried egg*
habit*

1 hobbies and everyday activities

Match the following verbs and phrases. The first one is done for you.

1 drive	**a** French	**1** ....f....
2 cook	**b** a meal	**2** ....
3 paint	**c** the piano	**3** ....
4 type	**d** a letter	**4** ....
5 sing	**e** awake	**5** ....
6 read	**f** a car	**6** ....
7 speak	**g** a picture	**7** ....
8 give	**h** me a game	**8** ....
9 play	**i** a song	**9** ....
10 listen to	**j** television	**10** ....
11 watch	**k** music	**11** ....
12 stay	**l** a record	**12** ....

2 what, where, what . . . like, how, how often

Put one of the question words or phrases in the blanks.

1 .... can I buy a stamp? – At the post office.

2 .... does Mabel travel to work? – By taxi.

3 .... does Mabel look ....? – She's a tall woman with blond hair and green eyes.

4 .... does Mabel go on holiday? – About four times a year.

5 .... is Mabel's house? – Near the station.

6 .... does Mabel have for breakfast? – Fried eggs.

7 .... does Mabel take exercise? – Never.

8 .... does Mabel do? – She's a businesswoman.

3 present simple and frequency adverbs

Rewrite the following sentences using the correct form of the verb and including the adverb.

Example: **usually** Peter (*go*) to the cinema on Saturday evenings

Peter usually goes to the cinema on Saturday evenings.

1 **always** Peter (*have*) coffee for breakfast

....

2 **usually** Mary and Emma (*go*) to Spanish classes on Tuesdays and Thursdays

....

3 **never** Peter (*get*) to work late

....

4 **usually** Mary and Emma (*watch*) the news on television

....

5 **sometimes** Peter (*play*) darts on Friday evenings

....

4 punctuation: question marks, capitals, full stops

Rewrite the following sentences putting in capitals, question marks (?) or full stops (.) where necessary.

Example: does simon play the guitar well

Does Simon play the guitar well?

1 where do mary and emma have lunch on sundays

....

2 you can see a good play at the majestic theatre

....

3 which is the platform for london

....

4 i usually eat at the mayfair restaurant

....

5 do i like paella yes i like it very much

....

5 frequency of activities

Complete the following sentences about you.

1 On Sundays I ....

2 Every Monday I ....

3 I .... once or twice a week.

4 I usually .... in the evening.

5 I always ....

6 read and write

NAME: Teresa Branco
AGE: 45
DESCRIPTION: She is a tall, thin woman with long black hair and brown eyes.
HABITS: She goes to the tennis club three times a week and she has lessons from Manuel da Silva. Mrs Branco plays tennis well. She always has lunch at the Caravela restaurant with her friend Emilia on Fridays. She sometimes has lunch at the tennis club with Jorge de Sousa. She never speaks to the manager of the club (Fernando Soares): they are not friends.
SIGNED: ....

EE Detective Agency

Look at this information about Teresa's husband and fill in the form about him.

Julio Branco . . . 56 . . . tall . . . grey hair, blue eyes . . . office every day . . . sauna twice a week . . . once a week squash with a colleague . . . badly . . . once a week squash with his secretary . . . sometimes lunch with his secretary . . . usually goes to work by car

NAME:
AGE:
DESCRIPTION:

HABITS:

SIGNED: ....

EE Detective Agency

13 Classwork

Interaction

1

In this mime game one student mimes an action; the others have to guess what it is. The student who guesses correctly gets a point. At the end of the game the student with the most points wins.

2

Student **A**: Look at number 7 on page 78. Complete the chart by asking **B** questions.
Student **B**: Look at number 7 on page 84. Complete the chart by asking **A** questions.
Do not look at each other's charts until you have finished.

Listening and acting out

1

Listen to the cassette and answer the questions.

1. Where is Judith?
2. Who is paying for the call?
3. How is George feeling?
4. What is George doing?

2

Put the correct names, Tony, Jane, Martin and George under the pictures.

....

3

Student **A** rings home. Student **A** asks student **B**:
- how she/he is feeling
- how the other people in the house are
- what they are doing

Language summary

New language items

What's [Mike] doing?
(= What is)
– He's [making coffee].
(= He is)

What are [Ron and Kate] doing?
– They're [peeling potatoes].
(= They are)

Is she [nursing] right now?
– Yes, she is./No, she isn't.

Are they acting right now?
– Yes, they are./No, they aren't.

What's the matter? Why don't you [take it to a vet]?
– Perhaps I will.

I am sailing
you are sailing
he / she / it } is sailing
we are sailing
you are sailing
they are sailing

New vocabulary/expressions * Activity Book vocabulary

In the kitchen
recipe
vegetable
omelette
to fry
pan
ingredients
peppers
plate
to chop
to taste
dish (= plate)
to peel

Leisure
to rest
to sail
to hitchhike
to climb
(swimming) pool
beach

Places
the Caribbean
the Alps
San Sebastian

Various
just
anyway
to put
extra
lovely
to smell
delicious
ready
oh dear!
to pick
floor
to wash
right now
painter
to lie
long
cool
drink
to stay
fantastic
to feel
terrible

perhaps
tooth
to ache
dentist
to limp
vet
watch
(to go) slow
jeweller's
electrician
radio
knee
to hurt
Christmas
I suppose
to pay*
call (*n*)*
to act*
sea*
ghost*

1 cooking verbs and food

Find the five verbs and two foods and put a line round them. One is done for you.

t	a	s	t	i	n	g	c	h
o	a	b	c	a	e	f	h	i
m	p	c	g	h	i	j	o	j
a	e	o	k	l	m	n	p	k
t	e	o	o	p	q	r	p	l
o	l	k	s	t	u	v	i	m
w	i	i	f	r	y	i	n	g
x	n	n	y	z	a	b	g	n
e	g	g	c	d	e	f	g	o

2 do/does, is/are -ing

Match the questions and answers. The first one is done for you.

1 What does Tom do?	**a** No, he isn't	**1** ...f...
2 Is Steve teaching right now?	**b** He acts in plays.	**2** ....
3 How does Mary get to work?	**c** Yes, she does.	**3** ....
4 What does Steve teach?	**d** Yes, he is. He's playing Hamlet.	**4** ....
5 What is Mary doing right now?	**e** She drives her car.	**5** ....
6 Is Tom acting at this moment?	**f** He teaches English.	**6** ....
7 Does Mary drive a bus?	**g** She's driving her bus.	**7** ....

3 is/are -ing

Write the correct form of the verb.

Example: He (*not paint*) ...isn't painting... right now.

1 Steve (*swim*) .... in the sea right now.

2 Tom and Nigel (*not climb*) .... right now.
They (*have*) .... breakfast.

3 Joan (*make*) .... coffee right now.
She (*not swim*) .... with Steve.

4 Mary (*sail*) .... in the Caribbean right now.
She (*not drive*) .... her bus.

5 Chris and Sharon (*not watch*) .... a film right now.
They (*listen to*) .... the radio.

6 Steve (*not teach*) .... right now.

4 revision

In the following sentences choose the correct alternative, **a** or **b**.

Example: I **a** were / **b** was in London. ...b...

1 What's John like? He's a **a** tall man. / **b** man tall. ....

2 John **a** work / **b** works in an office. ....

3 The post office is **a** next / **b** next to the station. ....

4 John can **a** swims. / **b** swim. ....

5 I **a** watch usually / **b** usually watch television. ....

5 description and commentary

Look at the two pictures. Write a paragraph about each.
What is happening? What are the people like?

In the first picture ....

....

....

....

....

In the second picture ....

....

....

....

....

Interaction

1

Look at the photographs and discuss them like the policemen. Say what you think the people are doing and what they have got in their hands, etc. You can see the photographs better on page 87.

2

Ask students questions to complete the chart.

FIND SOMEONE WHO:

- **a** was at a film yesterday evening ....
- **b** can't play chess ....
- **c** doesn't like classical music ....
- **d** has got two brothers ....
- **e** sometimes plays the guitar ....
- **f** hasn't got a dog ....
- **g** likes ice cream ....
- **h** always has coffee for breakfast ....
- **i** wasn't at home yesterday afternoon ....
- **j** has got a car ....

Listening and acting out

1

Listen to the cassette and choose the correct answer **a**, **b** or **c**.

1 Maggie and John are in **a** Mexico City. **b** Acapulco. **c** London.

2 Maggie wants **a** vegetable soup. **b** gazpacho. **c** mushroom soup.

3 Today is **a** Maggie's birthday. **b** John's birthday. **c** the waiter's birthday.

2

Listen to the cassette again. Answer the questions.

1 Does Maggie like the restaurant?
2 What is the date of Maggie's birthday?
3 Where did John see the date of Maggie's birthday?
4 What does John ask Maggie?

3

You are at a restaurant with a friend. Find out what your friend wants and then give the order to the waiter.
Ask your friend how he or she is getting on, etc.
Have a good meal!

Language summary

New language items

Has [the man] got a [passport]/ any [gloves] in his [briefcase]?
– Yes, he has./ No, he hasn't. (= has not)

What have you got in your [bag]?
– I've got my [matches]. (= I have)

They haven't got any [glue] but they've got some [sellotape].

Would you like some [tea]?
– I'd prefer some [coffee], if you've got any.
How do you take it?

I have got
you have got
he / she / it } has got
we have got
you have got
they have got

New vocabulary and expressions * Activity Book vocabulary

Newspapers/ newsagent's
newsagent
The Times
The Guardian
Time Magazine

Stationery
ballpoint (pen)
felt-tip (pen)
paper clip
staple
correcting fluid
eraser

Food and drink
butter
sugar
milk

Various
bookshop
to sell
any
passport
gun
bag
briefcase
pocket
item
store
lion
tiger
in stock
report
ending
branch
kind
Irish
only
both
without
to prefer
population
capital
industry
map
descent
hand*
gazpacho*
soup*
to marry*
to die*
us*
hut*
snow*
snowmobile*
broken*
to use*
heating oil*
fresh*

1 vocabulary: food

Look at the following words and then put them in the correct column. The first one is done for you. Write any other words that you can think of.

aubergines omelette butter
spaghetti roast beef cheese
steak potatoes onions
peppers minced meat

Vegetable	*Egg*	*Milk*	*Meat*	*Pasta*
aubergines				

2 some, any

Put *some* or *any* in the blanks.

1 The bookshop has not got .... newspapers.

2 The man has got .... cigarettes in his briefcase.

3 Has the woman got .... cigarettes in her handbag?

4 They have not got .... pencils in the stationery shop.

5 Have they got .... ballpoint pens?

6 They have got .... correcting fluid.

3 word order

Put the following words, phrases, and punctuation in the correct order to make sentences or questions. Use capital letters where necessary.

Example: | in hong kong | . | yesterday | I was |

I was in Hong Kong yesterday.

1 | I | where | a newspaper | buy | can | ? |

....

2 | peter | right now | is | ? | a new book | writing |

....

3 | right now | emma and mary | not | are | to the radio | . | listening |

....

4 | the man | has | in his briefcase | ? | got | a lighter |

....

5 | they | but | any glue | they | not | have got | . | some | sellotape | got | have |

....

4 'have got', description

Write five sentences about these three pictures. Say what the people look like and what they have got.

1 ....

2 ....

3 ....

4 ....

5 ....

5 read and write

You are on a desert island. Write a note for help to put in the bottle! Here are some notes to help you.

small island . . . dying . . . no food . . . some fresh water . . . all lying under the trees . . . very weak . . .

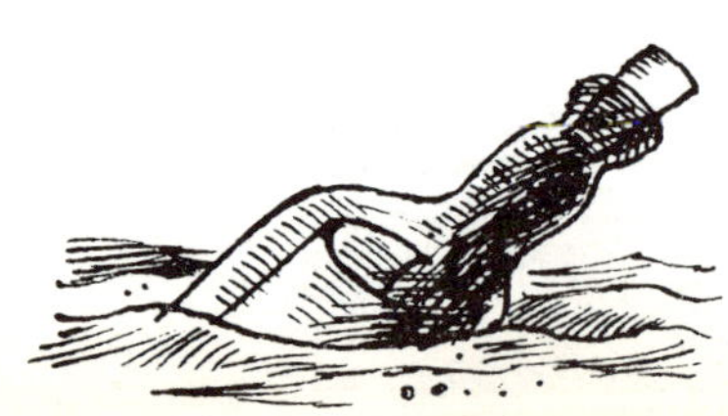

15 Classwork

Interaction

1

In pairs put the following sentences in the correct order to make a dialogue. (The first one is done for you.)

1 Good morning.

Here you are.

Yes.

London?

Well, there are two trains every hour, one at twenty past and one at twenty to.

How much is a return ticket?

Thank you. Here's your ticket and your change.

Oh, yes please. When do trains go to London?

Certainly sir. That will be fifteen pounds sixty.

Thanks.

Fifteen pounds sixty pence.

Good morning. Can I help you?

O.K. Can I have a return then, please?

2

Student **A**: Look at number 8 on page 79.
Complete the chart by asking student **B**.
Student **B**: Look at number 8 on page 85.
Complete the chart by asking student **A**.
Do not look at each other's charts until you have finished.

Listening and acting out

1

Listen to the cassette and answer the questions.

1 Who is selling the house, the man or the woman?
2 How many rooms has the house got?
3 How much is the house, according to the newspaper?
4 How much is the house, according to the woman?

2

Listen to the cassette again and write the correct numbers.

Bedrooms ....

Bathrooms ....

Acres (of land) ....

Swimming pools ....

3

Student **B** is selling his/her house.
Student **A** wants information about the house.
Student **A** rings up student **B**. Student **A** should ask about the numbers of bedrooms/bathrooms, etc.

Language summary

New language items

Are there any [rivers] in [the Isle of Man]?
– Yes, there are [four]./No, there aren't.
(= are not)

Is there any [agriculture] in [the Isle of Man]?
– Yes, there is./No, there isn't.
(= is not)

How many [tomatoes] are there?
– There { are a lot. / aren't many/any.

How much [sugar] is there?
– There { is a lot. / isn't much/any.

I'd like a ticket for [eight o'clock].
– Let's see. That's fine. Will you pay by cheque or in cash?

New vocabulary/expressions * Activity Book vocabulary

Geographical/ urban features
river
lake
mountain
village
airport
oil
coal
agriculture
market
region
bridge
heavy traffic
music hall
acre*
land*
natural resources*

energy*
industrial*
nation*

Travel agency
timetable
information
to pay { in cash / by cheque / by credit card

Various
how many
to talk
nice
to prepare
big
right
mushroom

a lot
petrol
litre
gosh!
detail
progress
ago
entertainment
fine
to clean
violin
accident
victim
to state
injury
to consist of
according to*
adventure*
kilo*

fridge*
rich*
over*
million*
important*
possible*
such*
serious*
unemployed*
business*
to close*

Places
the Isle of Man
Scotland*
Northern Ireland*
Wales*

1 geographical information

Study the map. Put each of the following words in one of the blanks. One is done for you.

airport
oil
village
town
bridge
mountain
coal
river
factory

....

village

....

....

....

....

....

....

....

2 revision

Match the questions and the answers. The first one is done for you.

1 Have you got any paper clips?	a I go swimming.	1 h
2 How much chalk is there?	b About twice a week.	2 ....
3 Are there any rivers in the Isle of Man?	c I like adventure films best.	3 ....
4 How often do you play squash?	d Yes, there is.	4 ....
5 What do you do on Sundays?	e At the newsagent's.	5 ....
6 How many brothers have you got?	f Yes, I can.	6 ....
7 Where can I buy a newspaper?	g Two.	7 ....
8 What's your favourite kind of film?	h No, I haven't.	8 ....
9 Is there any agriculture near your town?	i Yes, there are four.	9 ....
10 Can you play chess?	j There are three boxes.	10 ....

3 there is, there are

Put *is* or *are* in the blanks.

1 There .... some cheese on the table.
2 .... there any sausages in the supermarket?
3 There .... five kilos of tomatoes in the kitchen.
4 .... there any margarine in the fridge?
5 There .... not any honey in the grocery.

4 how much, how many

Write *how much* or *how many* in the blanks.

1 .... sisters have you got?
2 .... orange juice is there on the table?
3 .... petrol is there in the car?
4 .... erasers have you got?
5 .... cars can you see?

5 there is/there are, has got/have got

Read this passage and fill in the blanks with *one word* only.

The United Kingdom consists of England, Scotland, Northern Ireland and Wales. The UK [1]........ got a population of about 60 million. The UK is very rich in natural energy resources. There [2]........ a lot of oil in the North Sea and [3]........ lot of coal all over Britain (England, Scotland and Wales). The UK is an industrial nation but it has [4]........ serious problems. [5]........ are over four million unemployed, and many businesses are closing.

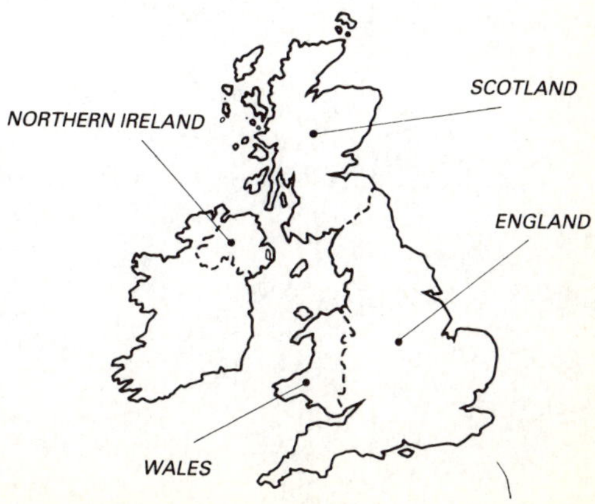

6 look and write

Look at the map and the information. Write a paragraph about the country.

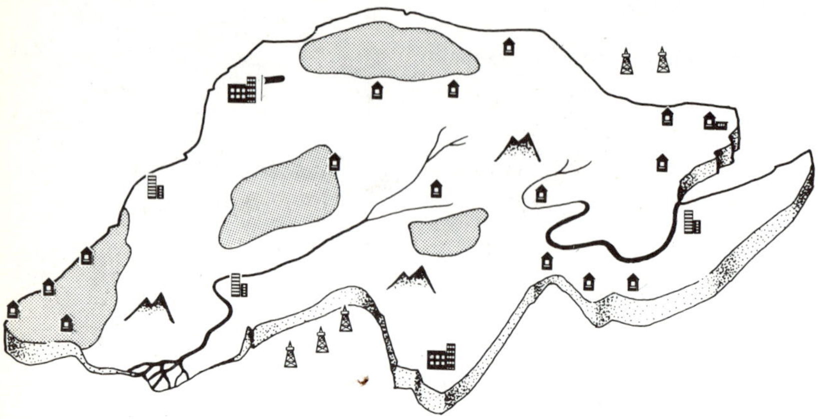

Name: TORTUGA

Population: 1.5 MILLION

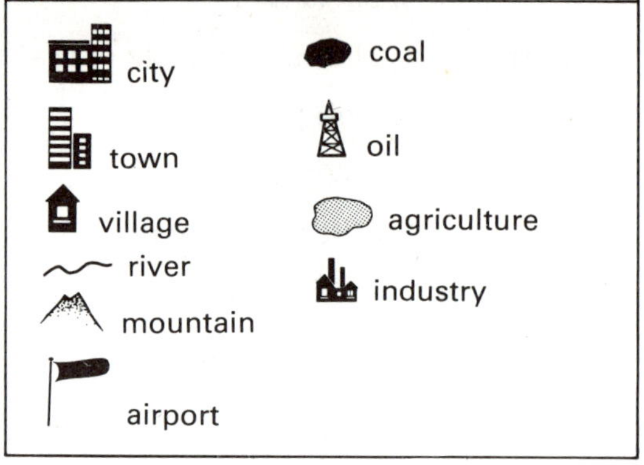

....

....

....

....

....

Now write a similar paragraph about your country.

Interaction

1 :

Fill in the calendar about your partner's activities next week. Ask what he or she is going to do and record the answers.

MONDAY	morning
	afternoon
	evening
TUESDAY	morning
	afternoon
	evening
WEDNESDAY	morning
	afternoon
	evening
THURSDAY	morning
	afternoon
	evening
FRIDAY	morning
	afternoon
	evening

2 ::

Look at the photographs and discuss them like the policemen. Say who you think the people are, what they have got and what they are going to do. You can see the photographs better on page 88.

Listening and acting out

1

Listen to the cassette and answer the questions.

1 Who is Ernest B. Gold?
2 When is the shuttle going to lift off?
3 What is the main objective of the mission?
4 What does Steve Terelli do well?

2

Complete the mission details.

MISSION DETAILS
Number of crew members: Men: ________
Women: ________

Main Objective: to ____________ supplies

Other tasks:

1 ____________________ radiation levels

2 ____________________ the moon

3

Student **A** is going on an expedition to either **a** the North Pole, or **b** the sea bed, or **c** a deserted island. Student **A** plans who is going to go on the expedition and what they are going to do.
Student **B** interviews student **A** about the expedition.

Language summary

New language items

What's [Tom] going to do in [March]?
(= What is)
– He's going to [get married].
(= He is)

Why is [Neil] wearing a [spacesuit]?
– Because he's going to [walk in space].

Where are you off to? You'd better [take light clothes].

What am I going to do?
What are you going to do?
What is {he / she / it} going to do?
What are we going to do?
What are you going to do?
What are they going to do?

New vocabulary/expressions * Activity Book vocabulary

Clothes
suit
shorts
leotard
apron
anorak
spacesuit
crash helmet

Places
the Solent
the Beaulieu Motor Museum
the New Forest
the Louvre
Guatemala City

Various
end
class
hard (work)
together
plan
to get married
to wear
because
to walk
space
to ride
motorbike
holiday
tour
during
sun
to travel
round
expensive
archaeology
the Maya
pyramid
through
exotic
seafood
umbrella
to rain
cold
to sunbathe
suntan oil
dark
hot
to catch
ferry
seasickness pills
rough
channel
to win
championship
star
same
director*
shuttle*
to lift off*
main objective*
crew*
member*
departure*
experiment*
university*
telephone*
family*
sky*
to deliver*
supplies*
radiation*
level*
the moon*
all*
chaotic*
to change*
job*
later*
to write*

1 vocabulary: clothes

Write the words from the list under the appropriate column. E.g. in column 1 write all the items of clothing that you can wear on the head.
You may need to use some words more than once.

shorts	trousers
leotard	shoes
apron	glasses
anorak	hat
skirt	coat
sweater	gloves
jacket	crash helmet
shirt	boots
dress	suit

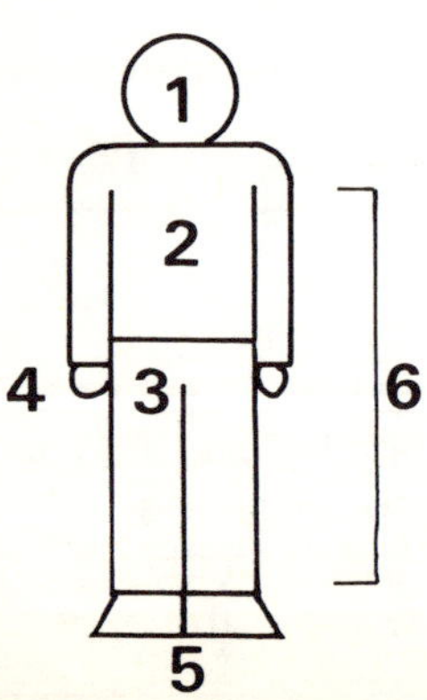

1	2	3
....	....	....
....	....	....
....	....	....
....	....	....
....	....	....
....	....	....

4	5	6
....	....	....
....	....	....
....	....	....
....	....	....
....	....	....
....	....	....

2 going to, is -ing

Write the correct form of the verb.

Example: Carmen (*wash*) .... is washing .... her hair right now.

1 Right now Carmen (*watch*) .... television at home.

2 Next Monday she (*see*) .... a new film with her boyfriend.

3 In May she (*travel*) .... to England.

4 In May, June and July next summer she (*study*) .... at an English university.

5 Now she (*talk*) .... to her boyfriend on the telephone.

6 Tomorrow morning she (*drive*) .... to her sister's house.

7 Tomorrow afternoon she (*play*) .... tennis with her sister.

8 Carmen's sister (*play*) .... the piano at a concert right now.

9 Right now Carmen's father (*wash*) .... the dishes.

10 Carmen (*cook*) .... a meal for the family next Sunday.

3 word order

Put the following words, phrases, and punctuation in order to make correct sentences or questions. Use capital letters where necessary.

Example: [in hong kong] [.] [yesterday] [I was]

I was in Hong Kong yesterday. ....

1 [the piano] [the guitar] [.] [can play] [antonio] [can't play] [but] [he]

....

2 [in] [any butter] [is] [the fridge] [?] [there]

....

3 [florida] [peter] [.] [next july] [to visit] [is going]

....

4 [industry] [the isle of man] [?] [how much] [there] [is] [in]

....

5 [mary and emma] [spanish classes] [go to] [how often] [?] [do]

....

4 conversation: offering advice

Complete the dialogue.

A: Where [1] .... off to?

B: [2] .... buy a newspaper.

A: You [3] .... take an umbrella.

B: Why?

A: Look at the sky! It [4] .... rain.

B: I know. But I [5] .... walk to the shop, I'm going to drive!

A: Oh! [6] .... buy a newspaper for me?

B: Yes, of course. Which is your [7] .... newspaper?

A: I [8] .... The Guardian [9] ....

B: Yes, I like The Guardian [10] .... I'll get you one.

5 going to

Complete the following sentences about you.

1 On Sunday I ....

2 I .... by car tomorrow.

3 I .... in July.

4 .... cook a meal.

5 In five minutes from now ....

6 read and write

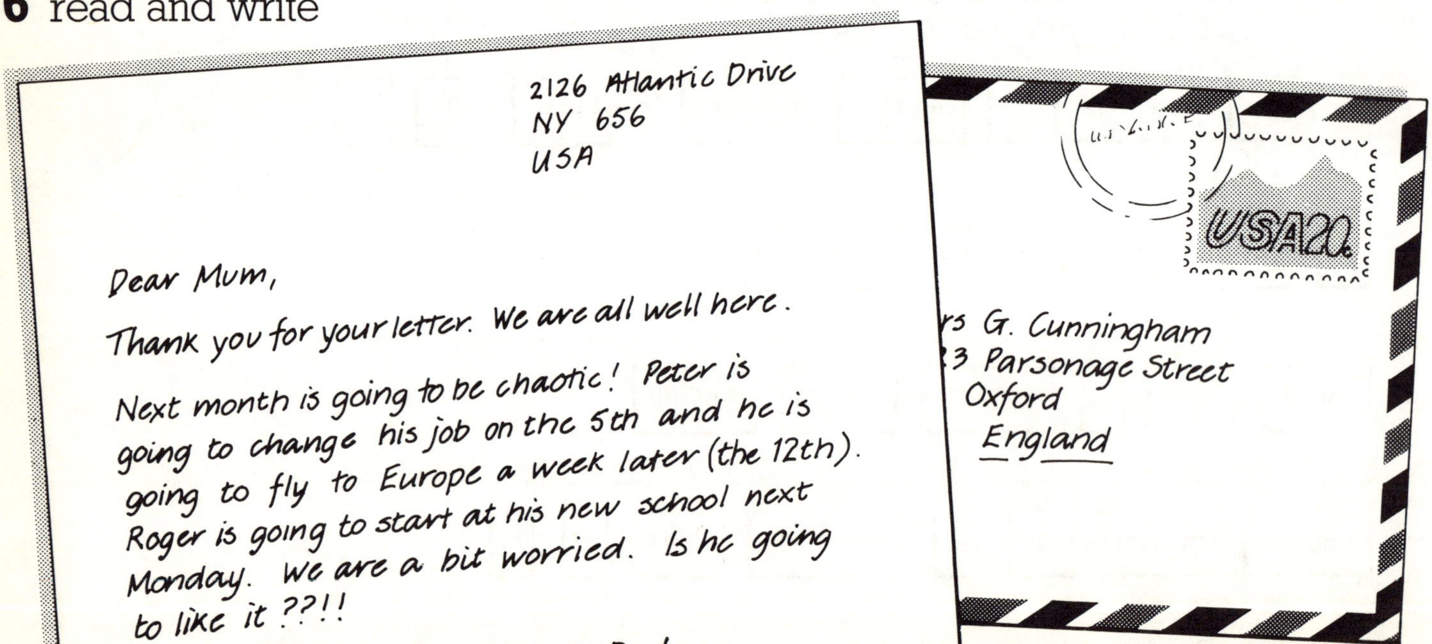

2126 Atlantic Drive
NY 656
USA

Dear Mum,

Thank you for your letter. We are all well here.

Next month is going to be chaotic! Peter is going to change his job on the 5th and he is going to fly to Europe a week later (the 12th). Roger is going to start at his new school next Monday. We are a bit worried. Is he going to like it ??!!

I'll write again soon. Love to Dad,

Lucy

Write a letter like Lucy's to an English-speaking friend. Say what you and members of your family are going to do in the near future.

17 Classwork

Interaction

1 ⁙

Ask other students questions to complete the chart.

FIND SOMEONE WHO:

1 took a photograph last week ....

2 fried an egg last weekend ....

3 wore a suit two days ago ....

4 went camping last year ....

5 collects stamps ....

6 always reads in bed ....

7 is going to watch television tonight ....

2 :

a Put the sentences in the correct order to make a dialogue. The first one is done for you.

1 What have you got in your hand?

For the film festival.

Why are you going to go there?

An airline ticket to Paris.

Do you always go to the Paris festival?

I bought a motorbike and drove to Montpellier in June.

No. Last year I didn't go to any festivals.

What did you do?

b Fill in these charts about the girl's two journeys with information from the dialogue.

LAST YEAR	***THIS YEAR***
Destination:	*Destination:*
Reason:	*Reason:*
Means of transport:	*Means of transport:*

Listening and acting out

1

Listen to the cassette and put these pictures (**a–f**) in the correct order in the box below.

1	2	3	4	5	6

2

Answer the questions.

1 What did Mrs Jones buy at the chemist's?
2 What was the car like?
3 How many men were there in the car
 a when it arrived? **b** when it drove away?
4 Why did the man with glasses fall down?
5 What did Mrs Jones do?

3

Student **A** saw the robbery. Student **B** is the policeman.
Student **A** tells the policeman about the robbery.

Study section

Language summary

New language items

What did [Sofia] do
[on Monday morning]?
– She [went shopping].

Did [Jane] [write a report]?
– Yes, she did./No, she didn't.
(= did not)

What did she [write], then?

What did you think of the [play]?
– I thought it was [boring].
So did I.
I didn't. I thought it
was [good].

What did I do? I screamed.
What did you do? You screamed.
What did he do? He screamed.
What did she do? She screamed.
What did it do? It screamed.
What did we do? We screamed.
What did you do? You screamed.
What did they do? They screamed.

New vocabulary/expressions * Activity Book vocabulary

Verbs: infinitive and past (regular)
happen, happened
push, pushed
scream, screamed
stop, stopped
listen, listened
visit, visited
cook, cooked
watch, watched

Verbs: infinitive and past (irregular)
do, did
put, put
drive, drove
get, got
throw, threw
buy, bought
go, went
read, read
think, thought

Adjectives of opinion
great
awful

Various
whole
story
into
hour
face
cliff
shopping
medical
journal
ballet
local
towards
I'll write
show
science fiction
anything
money
aspirin*
to camp*
to collect*
festival*
rail*
reason*
means of transport*
to drive away*
robbery*
bowl*
tennis player*
arm*
ladder*
to fall down*
plaster*
to take off*

1 past tense, present simple

Write the correct form of the verb. *Example*: Yesterday I (*go*) ....went........ to the shops.

1 Every day Jane (*go*) .... to work by car.

2 Yesterday morning she (*get*) .... up late.

3 Jane's car (*not start*) .... yesterday morning.

4 Jane usually (*have*) .... lunch in the hospital canteen.

5 Yesterday she (*have*) .... lunch with her father in a restaurant.

6 Last week Jane and her boyfriend, Antonio, (*buy*) .... a new car.

7 Last Wednesday they (*drive*) .... to a village for lunch.

8 Jane sometimes (*cook*) .... a meal for Antonio.

9 Last night she (*make*) .... a fantastic paella.

2 past tense questions

Complete the following questions about Jenny.

1 Where ....? – She went to the cinema.

2 What .... last night? – She cooked moussaka.

3 What .... this morning? – She read the newspaper.

4 .... on television yesterday? – She watched the news.

5 .... to work? – She ran because she was late.

3 revision

In the following sentences choose the correct alternative, **a** or **b**.

Example: I **a** were / **b** was in London. b

1 Do you like football? Yes, I **a** like. / **b** do. ....

2 What is John doing? He **a** is watching / **b** watching television. ....

3 There **a** is / **b** are some sugar in the bowl. ....

4 How much **a** the pen is? / **b** is the pen? Forty-nine pence. ....

5 What **a** do / **b** does you do on Sundays? I go jogging. ....

4 revision

Read the following story and fill in the blanks with one word only.

Jimmy is a tennis player. He did [1].................................... play tennis today because he [2].................................... his arm two weeks ago. He was on a ladder in [3].................................... town library. He took a [4].................................... from the shelf but he fell down. A friend [5].................................... him to the hospital and they put his [6].................................... in plaster. Jimmy was in hospital for a week. He [7].................................... television and listened to the radio. [8].................................... thought it was very boring.

Now Jimmy is at home again, but he is not [9].................................... to play tennis for four weeks. They are going [10].................................... take the plaster off next Wednesday.

5 read and write

Last Friday Sofia Menotti went to Verona from her home in Padua to visit her grandmother. Look at the pictures and complete the story.

Here are some verbs you may want to use: *to open, to say, to watch, to cook, to stop, to put petrol in the car*. Finish the story in your own way.

....

....

....

....

....

....

....

....

18 Classwork

Interaction

1 ●●● ●●●

In two teams write ten general knowledge questions. Now team **A** asks team **B** a question. Team **B** gets a point if they can answer correctly. Then team **B** asks team **A**. The team with the most points wins the game.

2 ●● ●●

a Group **A**: Look at number 9 on page 79.
Group **B**: Look at number 9 on page 85.
Group **C**: Look at number 9 on page 87.
Group **D**: Look at number 9 on page 88.
Each group should write two sentences about their picture using the past tense. **A**

b Make new groups with students from groups **A**, **B**, **C** and **D**. Tell the story in sequence *without looking at the pictures.*

Listening and acting out

1

Listen to the cassette and put these pictures (**a–d**) in the correct order in the box below.

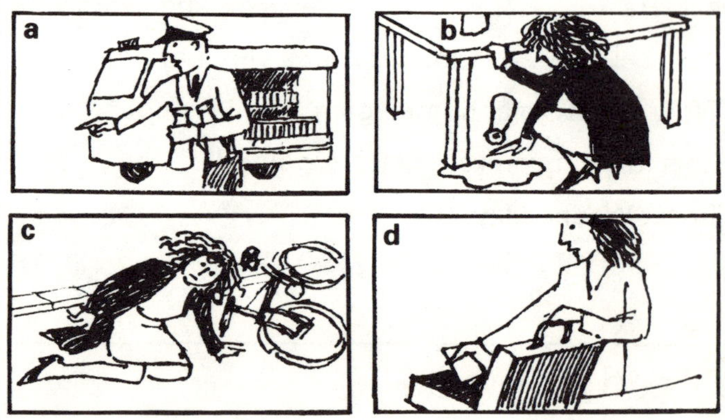

1	2	3	4

2

Answer the questions.

1 Who knocked on the door?
2 Who knocked the milk off the table?
3 Who ran into the road?
4 Who fell off her bicycle?
5 Who helped Janice off the ground?

3

Student **A** thinks of three things that happened that made her/him late. Student **A** arrives at **B**'s house late. **B** asks **A** what happened to her/him.

Language summary

New language items

Who [composed the Messiah]?
– (G. F. Handel].

Why is [Edmund Hillary] famous?
– Because he [climbed Everest].

When was he born?
– In [1919].
I've no idea.

I'm sorry I'm late.
– What happened to you?

Oh well!
It doesn't matter.
Not to worry.

New vocabulary/expressions * Activity Book vocabulary

Various
to survive
lucky
tree
to break
fall
to land
ledge
air-sea rescue
to rescue
helicopter
guy
to save
to kill
safe
to compose
to invent
to discover
to design
famous
apple
conqueror
writer
discoverer
radium
actress
climber
most
playwright
including
to return
place
example
to miss
to come in
party
to ring
on time
meeting
headache
busy
temple*
to bring*
rope*
to knock (on the door)*
to knock (the milk) off*
bicycle*
plane*
barrier*
come, came*
customs hall*
to shout*
shot*
cottage*
door*
bin*
sink*

Places and names
The Messiah
The Mousetrap
The Haywain
St. Paul's Cathedral
Mount Everest
Hamlet
Romeo and Juliet
Henry V
Twelfth Night
Emma
Mansfield Park
*Mona Lisa**

1 past tense endings: regular verbs

Put the following verbs in the correct column depending on the sound of their endings in the past tense. The first one for each column is done for you.

happen
scream
land
listen
compose
stop
visit
push
invent
discover
design
conquer
survive
save
kill
cook
watch

/d/	/t/	/ɪd/
happen - happened	push - pushed	visit - visited

2 questions and answers in the past

Match the questions and answers. The first one is done for you.

1 Who wrote Don Quixote?	**a** In 1564.	**1** ......C......
2 What did Columbus do in 1492?	**b** He wrote music.	**2** ....
3 Why is Cervantes famous?	**c** Cervantes.	**3** ....
4 Where did Napoleon die?	**d** Because he was president of the USA.	**4** ....
5 When was Shakespeare born?	**e** No, he didn't.	**5** ....
6 Did Lauren Bacall marry Humphrey Bogart?	**f** Michaelangelo.	**6** ....
7 Did Shakespeare write Evita?	**g** On the island of Elba.	**7** ....
8 Why is Kennedy famous?	**h** Because he wrote Don Quixote.	**8** ....
9 Who painted the Sistine Chapel?	**i** He discovered America.	**9** ....
10 What did Beethoven do?	**j** Yes, she did.	**10** ....

3 auxiliary verbs: be, do, can, have

Put one of the auxiliary verbs (*be, do, can* or *have*) in the blanks.
Be, do or *have* may be in the present or past tense.

1 .... you going to visit your grandmother tomorrow? No, I'm not.

2 .... you play chess in the evenings? – Yes, sometimes.

3 .... you watch television last night? – No, I did not.

4 .... I buy a camera in this shop? – Yes, what kind would you like?

5 .... you got any films for the camera? – Yes.

6 .... Steve and Joan visit Germany? – No, they visited France and Spain.

7 .... Tom and Nigel climb mountains every year? – No, not always.

8 .... Antonio speak Portuguese? – Yes, of course.

9 .... Pedro go to the United States last year? – Yes, for three months.

10 .... you got any shorts? – Yes . . . blue and white ones.

4 word order

Put the following words, phrases and punctuation in order to make correct sentences and questions. Use capital letters where necessary.

Example: [in hong kong] [yesterday] [.] [I was]

I was in Hong Kong yesterday. ....

1 [to the cinema] [last night] [john] [?] [go] [did]

....

2 [any cheese] [she has got] [.] [she has not got] [but] [some butter]

....

3 [in bed] [but] [not sleeping] [.] [atsuko] [is] [she is]

4 [sunday morning] [john] [last] [do] [what] [?] [did]

5 [to the university] [yesterday] [carmen did not] [,] [she went] [.] [go to the beach]

5 read and write

Read this extract from the book *To Kill in Kowloon* by Geoffrey Bridger.
Now look at Geoffrey Bridger's notes for the first chapter of his new book *To Kill at Home*. Use the notes to write the beginning of the chapter.

Chapter 1: The airport

At ten o'clock in the morning a plane landed at Kowloon airport and a tall man with fair hair and blue eyes got out and walked towards the airport buildings.

There was a beautiful Chinese girl at the barrier. She looked at all the passengers as they came out of the customs hall. Suddenly she screamed, 'Gregory, Gregory. I'm over here!' The tall man looked at her and ran towards her. 'My Ling,' he shouted.

There was a shot and the man fell to the ground.

Chapter 1 - The Cottage

car - 11.30 p.m. - cottage
tall woman - blond hair
table - plate of spaghetti
spaghetti - plate - in the bin
made some coffee - watched TV
man looked through window
screamed

19 Classwork

Interaction

1

In pairs put the following cards in the correct order to make a dialogue. The first one is done for you.

1 Do you like your job?

Well anyway, would you like a cup of coffee?

It's exhausting. I have to wash the floors, clean the windows, empty the ashtrays . . .

No, I don't.

Oh, I don't know. I'd like to travel . . . and I want to study.

Why not?

No, I don't think so. I can't afford to.

Well what would you like to do instead?

Are you going to leave this job then?

Yes, please. That would be great!

2

Complete the chart by interviewing your partner.

NAME: ....

AGE: ....

OCCUPATION: ....

OBLIGATIONS: ....

at home ....

at school/college/work

....

PLANS/AMBITIONS (what would he or she like to do in the future?):

....

Listening and acting out

1

Listen to the cassette and say whether the following statements are true or false.

1 Anne is an athlete.
2 Jo is a marathon runner.
3 Anne doesn't want to make a parachute jump.
4 Jo makes a parachute jump every day.

2

Listen to the cassette again and answer the questions.

1 How often does Anne train?
2 How far does Anne run in training?
3 When is the marathon race?
4 When is Jo's first jump?

3

In pairs have a similar conversation. Student **A** invites student **B**.
Student **B** says 'No . . . I have to . . .'
Student **A** tries to persuade student **B** (like Jo on the cassette). **B** continues to make excuses.

Language summary

New language items

What does [Lucy] have to do?
– She has to [make the beds].
What would [Lucy] like to do?
– She'd like to [meet the president].

What's the matter with [the man]?
– He has to [go to the office party] but he doesn't want to [meet the boss's wife].

Would you like to [come for a drink]?
– I can't, I'm afraid.
What about tomorrow?
– That would be great.

New vocabulary/expressions * Activity Book vocabulary

Various
something
the States
to come round
to pack
to meet
bed
the world
president
letter
telephone
philosophy
customer
to get cold
to get wet
office
boss
diplomat
thing
cocktail party
polite
to retire
Africa
to collect
butterfly
actually
to phone
rhino
female
baby
horn
powder
to afford*
to empty*
ashtray*
instead*
obligation*
ambition*
marvellous*
to enjoy yourself*
to smile*
to participate*

1 vocabulary: collocations

Match the following verbs and phrases. The first one is done for you.

1 wash	**a** for a meal	**1** ....b....
2 answer	**b** my hair	**2** ....
3 make	**c** exercise	**3** ....
4 miss	**d** the telephone	**4** ....
5 take	**e** Naples	**5** ....
6 get	**f** the bus	**6** ....
7 visit	**g** to Naples	**7** ....
8 come	**h** the beds	**8** ....
9 drive	**i** married	**9** ....

2 question words: what, where, why, how, who, how often

Put one of the question words or phrases in the blanks.

1 .... is Dimitri wearing an apron? – He's going to cook a meal.
2 .... is Jane doing right now? – She's reading a medical journal.
3 .... does Mario play squash? – About once a week.
4 ....did Steve and Joan go to Spain? – By car.
5 .... got wet last night? – Atsuko did.
6 .... does Lucy play cards? – In the Bridge Club.
7 .... does Jane want to do? – She wants to get married.
8 .... does Dimitri watch television? – Every evening.
9 .... did Peter go last September? – To Acapulco.

3 have to, want to

Put the correct form of the verb using either *want to* or *have to*.

Example: Jane (*get married*) wants to get married but Antonio does not.

1 Sylvie (*get up*) .... at six o'clock every morning. She does not like it.

2 Steve and Joan (*visit*) .... Turkey for their holiday next year.

3 Sofia (*learn*) .... Greek. She has got a Greek boyfriend.

4 Peter and Lucy (*go*) .... to a party tonight but they are not happy about it.

5 Caroline (*make*) .... beds at the hospital and she does not like it.

4 revision

Read the passage and fill in the blanks with one word only.

Caroline Gordon is not happy [1]........................ the hospital where she is [2]........................ nurse. She does not [3]........................ the work and she thinks [4]........................ is boring. Every day she has [5]........................ make beds, feed the patients [6]........................ write reports. This afternoon Caroline [7]........................ going to ring her friend and [8]........................ are going to talk about [9]........................ holidays. Last year they went [10]........................ the Alps but they [11]........................ not know where to go this year. [12]........................ and her friend like climbing [13]........................ Caroline climbs very well.

The only problem is that Caroline [14]........................ go on a [15]........................ expensive holiday. She has not [16]........................ a lot of money.

At [17]........................ moment Caroline is talking to [18]........................ patient, but she is thinking about her [19]........................ She [20]........................ to leave the hospital right now, but she has still got two hours left at work.

5 read and write

Read this:

Is your life boring? Are you always exhausted?

We can help you!

Listen to previous Club Aegean guests.

'I loved it! Club Aegean was exciting!'
Hilda Blank, London.

'It was fantastic! Lots of sun.'
Jeff Tomson, Oxford.

'Club Aegean was marvellous. I met my husband there!'
Meryl Irons, Los Angeles.

What do you have to do to go on holiday at Club Aegean?

* Fill in the coupon below and send it, with a 10% deposit, to Club Aegean, Inc. 276354 North Street East # 492, Bayou Canyon, Nevada.

AEGEAN

I would like to go to the Club Aegean from (*date*)

__________ to __________ 19____

I enclose a 10% deposit. Please send me more details.

Name: __________

Address: __________

Signed: __________ Date: __________

Write a similar advertisement for one of the following:

a a cruise ship
b a wildlife safari
c a language school

20 Classwork

Interaction

1 •••

1 Write a different word in each square below.
2 Divide into two teams.
3 A member from team **A** chooses a number from 1–16.
4 A member from team **B** says his word for that number.
5 The member from team **A** uses that word in a sentence or question and gets a point if he or she uses it correctly.

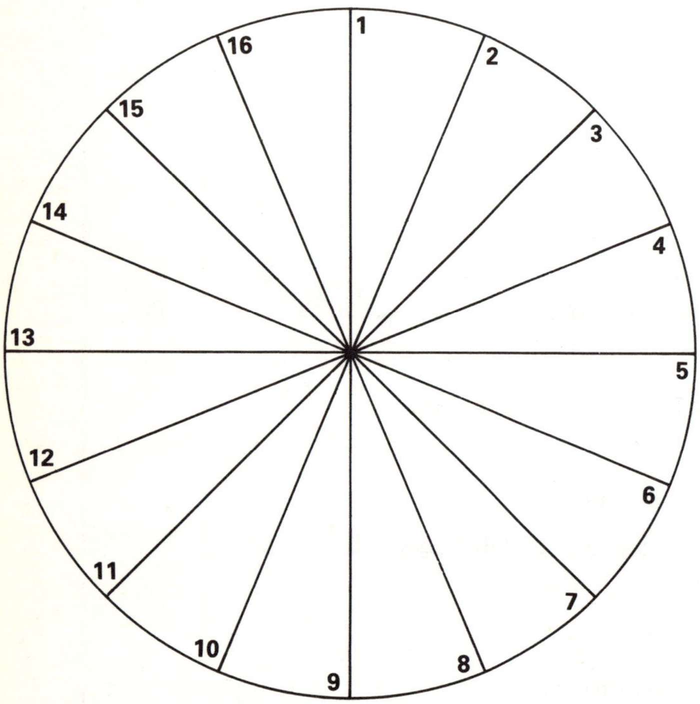

2 •

Student **A**: Look at number 10 on page 80. Complete the text with information that **B** has.
Student **B**: Look at number 10 on pages 86. Complete the text with information that **A** has.
Do not look at each other's texts until you have finished.

Listening and acting out

1

Listen to the cassette and answer the questions.

1 Did Gerald like the exam?
2 Did Mick like the exam?
3 Did Gerald know Judy's name?
4 Is Gerald going to go to the party tonight?

2

Look at these questions from Gerald, Mick and Judy's exam. Listen to the cassette and then put the correct number for each question in the brackets.

ECONOMICS
Paper 2

Answer 3 questions.

(☐) Is the cost of medicine going to increase or decrease in the next twenty years?

(☐) What are the main uses of computers in the modern world?

(☐) The price of oil caused the world recession. Discuss.

(☐) What is the relationship between production and jobs in a recession?

(☐) Why is an increase in car production a problem?

3

You have just finished an exam. In small groups say if you liked the exam and arrange a party for tonight.

20 Study section

Language summary

New language items

He [fell off his bicycle], didn't he?

He's a [teacher], isn't he?

Why didn't [Sylvie] [write postcards]?
– Because she [read a book].

We enjoyed [having you].
– I'll give you a call.
We'll look forward to that.
– Not at all.

They are Spanish, aren't they?
She lives in Cambridge, doesn't she?
They are going to start their honeymoon, aren't they?
She broke her leg, didn't she?

New vocabulary/expressions * Activity Book vocabulary

Various
congratulations
mechanic
to be right
to arrest
already
to crash
to fall off
honeymoon
arm
leg
(to have) a heart attack
to be ready
postcard
to oversleep
to drop
sunburnt
permanent
temporary
duties
army
cook
description
future
recent
moustache
dislikes
everything

Social expressions
a lovely dinner
to invite
to give (you) a call
to be in touch
to hear from (you)
to look forward to
course
speaker
aspect
necessary
major
scientific
language
word
difference
vocabulary
production*
recession*
success*
to learn*
social activities*
to continue*
studies*
grammar*
textbook*
conversation*
month*

1 conversational expressions

The following expressions have all been mixed up! Find out what expressions there are among them and write them in the space provided. One is done for you.

~~I'll be~~ *take an umbrella.*	How do you *some coffee.*
I'll look forward *I'm late.*	I'd rather *to that.*
You'd better ~~*in touch.*~~	I'm sorry *some help?*
Thank you *talking to you.*	Do you want *not.*
We enjoyed *for inviting me.*	I'd prefer *take it?*

1 I'll be in touch.
2 ....
3 ....
4 ....
5 ....
6 ....
7 ....
8 ....
9 ....
10 ....

2 tag questions

Make the sentences into questions. *Example*: You are Australian, ...aren't you......?

1 Jane cannot speak Portuguese, ...?

2 Sofia is a tourist guide, ...?

3 Jane Austen wrote novels, ...?

4 Tom is going to get married, ...?

5 Steve and Joan are not teaching right now, ...?

6 Paul does not like octopus, ...?

7 Sofia drove to Naples, ...?

8 Peter Smith does not live in Washington, ...?

9 You are going to get wet, ...?

10 Jane did not write her report, ...?

3 revision

In the following sentences choose the correct alternative, **a** or **b**.

Example: I **a** were / **b** was in London. ......b......

1 There **a** aren't / **b** isn't any cheese in the cupboard. ....

2 My mother **a** she is / **b** is fifty-two years old. ....

3 Where **a** did you / **b** you did go yesterday? ....

4 I want to **a** swimming. / **b** swim. ....

5 **a** Did you / **b** Do you see your friend yesterday? ....

4 word order: punctuation

Put the following words, phrases and punctuation in order to make correct sentences and questions. Use capital letters where necessary.

Example: [in hong kong] [yesterday] [ ] [i was]

I was in Hong Kong yesterday.

1 [at six o'clock] [get up] [.] [every morning] [has to] [she]

....

2 [to the shops] [but] [peter] [get wet] [.] [does not want to] [has] [to] [he] [go] [.]

....

3 [a piano] [?] [their house] [peter and lucy] [got] [in] [have]

....

4 [between] [the hospital] [the bank] [is] [.] [and the station]

....

5 [caroline] [every day] [?] [what] [at work] [have to do] [does]

....

5 revision

Read the dialogue and fill in the blanks with one word only.

SHEILA: Hey, Sheila! 1.................................. look worried! What's 2.................................. matter?

MELANIE: I can't find my keys and I have 3.................................. be at the folk club in 4.................................. an hour.

SHEILA: 5.................................. you going to meet someone there?

MELANIE: No, I'm 6.................................. to sing.

SHEILA: How often do you 7.................................. at the club?

MELANIE: This is only the 8.................................. time. I sang there 9.................................. week.

SHEILA: Was it a success?

MELANIE: Yes, I 10.................................. so. Look, you can't see my keys, can you?

SHEILA: What about those ones 11.................................. the table?

MELANIE: Oh, yes! Thanks. I have to go. I'll 12.................................. you on Thursday for lunch.

6 read and write

Read these reports from students at a language school. The term has just finished.

I liked the English Course but it was very difficult for me. I wanted more grammar but the other students wanted more conversation, etc.

I think nearly all the teachers were good, but *not* Mr Rushton. He can *not* teach.

I am going to return to this school again

I want to speak good English.

My English class was very good and it was often very interesting. We had a lot of grammar (I like grammar) and I liked the textbook.

The teachers were nice – especially Mr. Rushton. I think he is excellent – very well-prepared. (He is also very good-looking).

My English course was great fun. I think I learnt a lot. My teachers were very good.

We had to study a lot at home and I did not like that! I did not have much time for social activities. I am going to continue my studies in Japan.

Write a report on your English classes.

A

1

Ask: What does ________ do? Where does ________ live? Where is ________ now?
Complete the form.

NAME	John	Anne	Tim	Sue
HOME		Liverpool		New York
OCCUPATION	policeman			nurse
NOW		at home	at school	

2

Ask:
Where does/do ________ live?
Ask about: Ken, Jane, Mark and Rose, Steve, David and Sue
Write their names on the map.

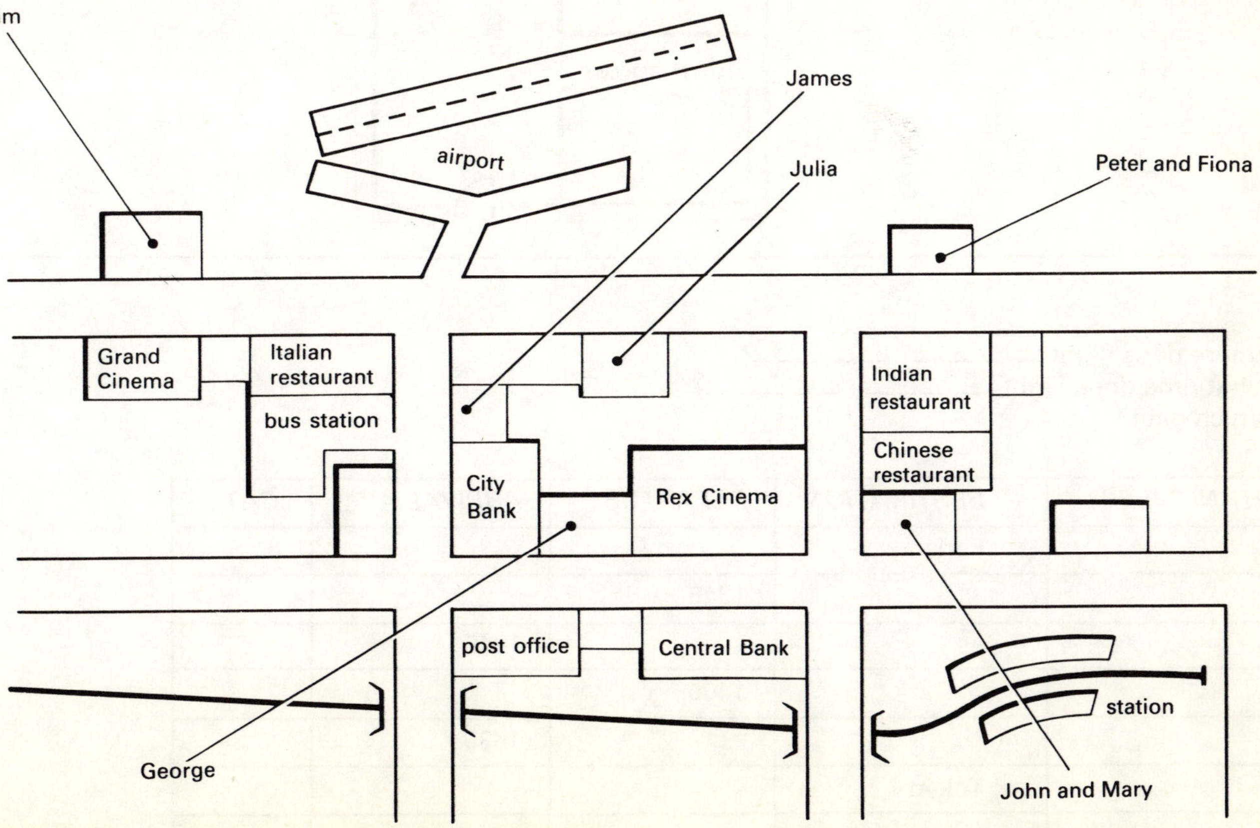

A

3

Ask: Where was/were ________ at ________ o'clock. Put the names on the plans.
Ask about: Peter, Katie, Mary and Laura

20:30 hrs

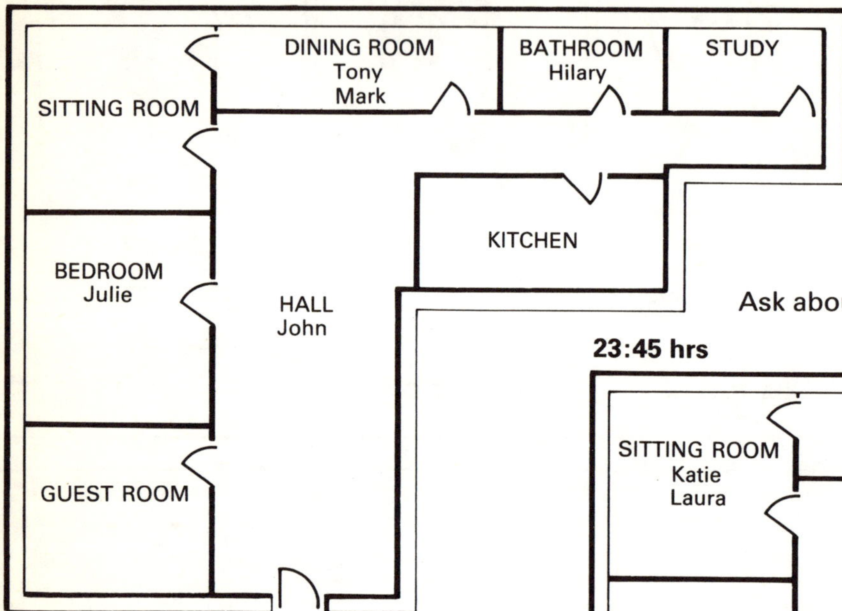

Ask about: John, Tony, Mark, Hilary

23:45 hrs

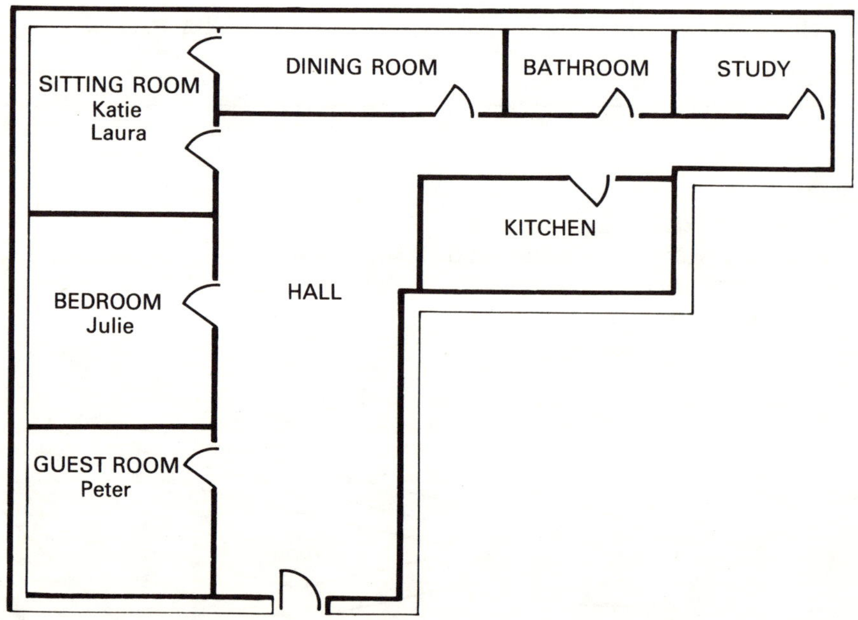

4

Ask: Where does flight ________ ________?
What time does flight ________ ________?
Which gate?

FLIGHT NUMBER	*DESTINATION*	*DEPARTURE*	*ARRIVAL (LT*)*	*GATE*
389	Paris			6
560		1345		
027			1645	
951		1400		2
006			1630	
323	Tokyo			
**LT = local time*				

A

5

1 Colour the man's shoes, trousers, sweater, eyes and hair (or write the colours).

2 Find at least four similarities with B's picture.

6

Ask: Does Tom like ________? Can Steve and Joan ________?

SPORT	Tom *likes*	*ability*	Steve and Joan *like*	*ability*
skiing				
skating	✓	✗	✗	✗
swimming				
boxing	✗	✗	✗	✗
(playing) golf				
(playing) baseball	✓	✗	✓	✗
(playing) tennis				
(playing) football	✓	✓	✗	✗

7

Ask: What does ________ do? How old is ________?
Is ________ ________ ing now? How often does ________ ________?

Fill in the chart.

NAME	Keith	Pauline	Tony and Pat	Diana and Kate	Richard and Roger
OCCUPATION	painter		singers		teachers
AGE			Tony: 19 Pat: 21		Richard: 39 Roger: 42
RIGHT NOW	jogging		swimming		watching a video film
FREQUENCY OF ACTIVITY			four/five times a week		twice a week

A

8

Ask:
How much ________ is there?
How many ________ are there?

ITEM	AMOUNT	ITEM	AMOUNT
tea		onions	60 kilos
coffee	50 kilos	tomatoes	
sugar		potatoes	110 kilos
		mushrooms	
milk	80 litres	aubergines	35 kilos
butter		carrots	
cheese	26 kilos		
eggs			

9

ELVIS PRESLEY

☆ King of Rock and Roll ☆

In any book about pop music you will find the name Elvis Presley. And in many textbooks for students of English his story is told. Why? Why is Elvis Presley so famous?

Elvis Presley sang rock and roll. His record .... (made in 1956) sold one million copies. He starred in many films and was the idol of singers like the Beatles and the Rolling Stones.

Elvis Presley was born on .... His parents were Vernon Presley and Gladys Smith. They lived in ...., Mississippi. In January 1942 Elvis' father gave him a .... and the young boy started to play.

In .... the Presley family went to live in Memphis, Tennessee. After school Elvis worked as a .... In 1953 Elvis went to Sun Records. He paid .... and recorded a song for his mother. A girl from the record company heard the song and Elvis made a record for them called *That's all right Mama.* It was a great success and Elvis was soon very famous.

In .... Elvis joined the United States Army and went to Germany. There he met a young girl called .... They were married in the United States on 1st May, 1967. They had a daughter called .... But Elvis was always away from home — in Hollywood or Las Vegas — and Priscilla was unhappy. They got divorced.

Elvis Presley died on 16th August, ..., but people have still not forgotten him. He changed pop music for ever.

B

1

Ask: What does ________ do? Where does ________ live? Where is ________ now?
Complete the form.

NAME	John	Anne	Tim	Sue
HOME	London		San Francisco	
OCCUPATION		housewife	student	
NOW	at work			at work

2

Ask:
Where does/do ________ live?
Ask about: Julia, John and Mary, George, Peter and Fiona, James
Write their names on the map.

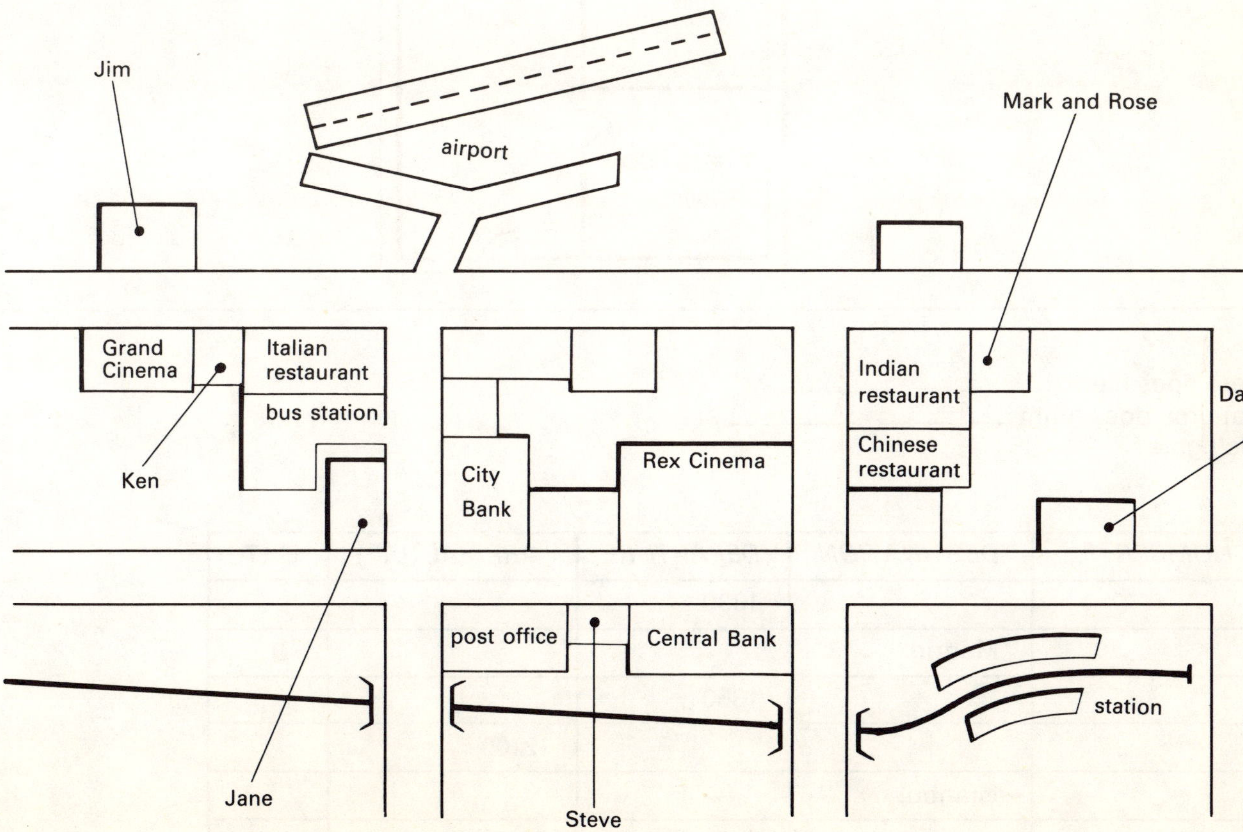

B

3

Ask: Where was/were ________ at ________ o'clock? Put the names on the plans.

Ask about: John, Hilary, Tony and Mark, Julie

20:30 hrs

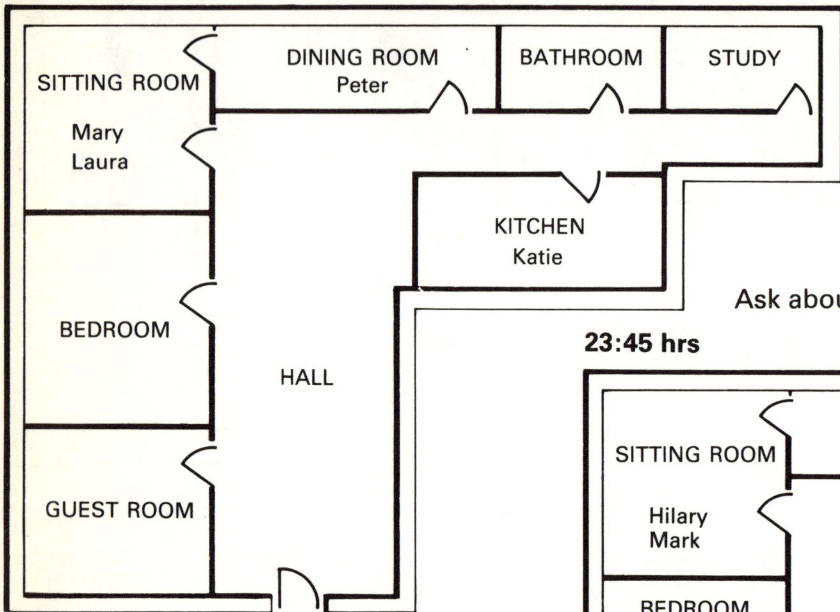

Ask about: Katie and Laura, Julie, Mary, Peter

23:45 hrs

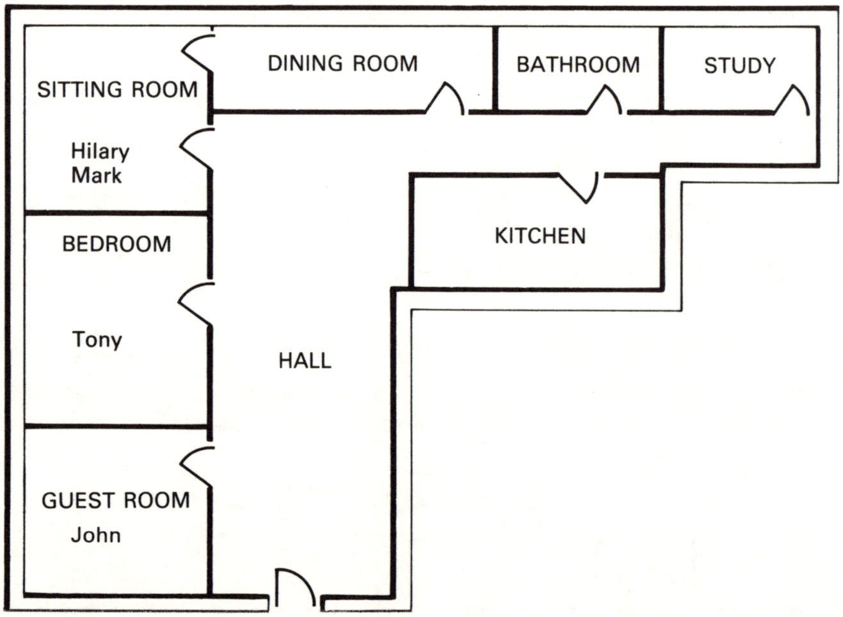

4

Ask: Where does flight ________ ________?
What time does flight ________ ________?
Which gate?

FLIGHT NUMBER	*DESTINATION*	*DEPARTURE*	*ARRIVAL (LT*)*	*GATE*
389		1330		
560	Madrid			9
027		1350		
951			2100	
006	Istanbul			
323		1425		13
**LT = local time*				

B

5

1 Colour the woman's shoes, trousers, sweater, eyes and hair (or write the colours).

2 Find at least four similarities with A's picture.

B

6

Ask: Does Tom like ________? Can Steve and Joan ________?

SPORT	**Tom** *likes*	*ability*	**Steve and Joan** *like*	*ability*
skiing 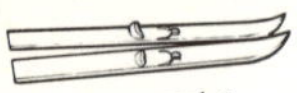	✓	✓	✗	✗
skating 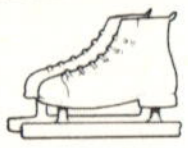				
swimming 	✓	✓	✓	✓
boxing 				
(playing) golf 	✓	✓	✗	✗
(playing) baseball 				
(playing) tennis 	✗	✗	✓	✗
(playing) football 				

7

Ask: What does ________ do? How old is ________?
Is ________ ________ing now? How often does ________ ________?

Fill in the chart.

NAME	**Keith**	**Pauline**	**Tony and Pat**	**Diana and Kate**	**Richard and Roger**
OCCUPATION		actress		dancers	
AGE	69	26		Diana: 22 Kate: 31	
RIGHT NOW		having a bath		dancing	
FREQUENCY OF ACTIVITY	every day	twice a day		every morning and five nights a week	

B

8

Ask:
How much ________ is there?
How many ________ are there?

ITEM	AMOUNT	ITEM	AMOUNT
tea	48 kilos	onions	
coffee		tomatoes	35 kilos
sugar	120 kilos	potatoes	
		mushrooms	56 kilos
milk		aubergines	
butter	42 kilos	carrots	40 kilos
cheese			
eggs	500		

9

ELVIS PRESLEY

☆ King of Rock and Roll ☆

In any book about pop music you will find the name Elvis Presley. And in many textbooks for students of English his story is told. Why? Why is Elvis Presley so famous?

Elvis Presley sang rock and roll. His record *Heartbreak Hotel* (made in . . . .) sold one million copies. He starred in many films and was the idol of singers like the Beatles and the Rolling Stones.

Elvis Presley was born on 8th January, 1935. His parents were Vernon Presley and . . . . They lived in Tupelo, Mississippi. In . . . . Elvis' father gave him a guitar and the young boy started to play.

In 1948 the Presley family went to live in . . . . , Tennessee. After school Elvis worked as a lorry driver. In . . . . Elvis went to Sun Records. He paid $4 and recorded a song for his . . . . A girl from the record company heard the song and Elvis made a record for them called . . . . It was a great success and Elvis was soon very famous.

In 1958 Elvis joined the United States Army and went to . . . . There he met a young girl called Priscilla. They were married in the United States on . . . . They had a daughter called Lisa Marie. But Elvis was always away from home — in Hollywood or Las Vegas — and Priscilla was unhappy. They got divorced.

Elvis Presley died on . . . . , 1977, but people have still not forgotten him. He changed pop music for ever.

C

4

Ask: Where does flight ________ ________?
What time does flight ________ ________?
Which gate?

FLIGHT NUMBER	*DESTINATION*	*DEPARTURE*	*ARRIVAL (LT*)*	*GATE*
389			1420	
560			1425	
027	Lisbon			3
951	Mexico City			
006		1415		11
323			0825	
**LT = local time.*				

9

See page 47

D

9

See page 55

Nationalities (*see page 11 exercise 1*)

-an	-ish	-ese	irregular
Mexican	English	Japanese	French
Puerto Rican	Spanish	Portuguese	Swiss
German	Danish	Chinese	Greek
American	Swedish		Dutch
Australian	Turkish		
Brazilian	Irish		
Saudi Arabian			
Peruvian			
Hungarian			
Italian			
Argentinian			
Belgian			
Yugoslavian			

Tapescript

ANNOUNCER: Activity Book Unit **1**. Listen.

(*Knocking on the door*)
DOCTOR: Come in.
(*Door opens, footsteps*)
Come in . . . ah . . . hello.
ANNE: Good morning doctor.
DOCTOR: Good morning. Please sit down.
ANNE: Thank you.
DOCTOR: Now . . . umm . . . what's your name?
ANNE: Anne Murray.
DOCTOR: Er . . . Murray . . . and what do you do?
ANNE: I'm a housewife.
DOCTOR: And . . . er, where do you live?
ANNE: Tarragona.
DOCTOR: Tarragona? Where's that?
ANNE: In Spain. I'm here on holiday.
DOCTOR: Oh, really? Now then, what seems to be the matter?

ANNOUNCER: Activity Book Unit **2**. Listen.

(*Phone rings and is picked up*)
CHARLOTTE: Hello.
CALLER: Hello. Is that Jane?
CHARLOTTE: No, this is Charlotte, her sister, speaking.
CALLER: Oh hello, Charlotte. This is Peter. How are you?
CHARLOTTE: Fine thanks, and you?
CALLER: I'm very well. Is Jane there?
CHARLOTTE: No, I'm afraid she isn't. She's at school.
CALLER: Oh dear . . . is your mother at home?
CHARLOTTE: No, she isn't. She's at work. But my father's at home. Do you want to speak to him?
CALLER: No, no thank you. I'll ring again. Bye.
CHARLOTTE: Bye.
(*Phone is put down*).

ANNOUNCER: Activity Book Unit **3**. Listen.

MAN: Hello!
GIRL: Hello.
MAN: Is your father at home?
GIRL: No.
MAN: Oh, really? Where is he?
GIRL: At the hospital.
MAN: At the hospital!
GIRL: Yes. He's a doctor.
MAN: Oh, I see. Where does he work?
GIRL: At the Radcliffe Hospital.
MAN: Oh yes, in Suffolk Street.
GIRL: No. It's on South Street opposite the cinema.
MAN: Oh yes, of course. But your mother's in.
GIRL: Oh no! She's at school.
MAN: Oh, I see. She's a teacher.
GIRL: No, she isn't. She's a secretary.
MAN: Oh dear . . .
GIRL: What do you do?
MAN: I'm a salesman. I sell encyclopaedias.
GIRL: Oh! Encyclopaedias? How boring! Goodbye!
(*Door slams*)
MAN: (*groans*) Back to the car . . .

ANNOUNCER: Activity Book Unit **4**. Listen.

(*Party noise*)
PATTY: Hello.
RAY: Hello. I'm Ray.
PATTY: I'm Patty. Where are you from Ray?
RAY: Here . . . London, England! What about you?
PATTY: I'm Australian.
RAY: Oh. What do you do . . . for a living I mean?
PATTY: I'm a designer. And before you ask, I live in London, I'm twenty-three and I'm not married.
RAY: Oh . . . er . . . well . . . I . . .
MIKE: Hey, Ray. Hello.
RAY: Mike. Hello. Good to see you. Mike, this is Patty. She's a designer from Australia, she lives in London, she's twenty-five . . .
PATTY: Twenty-*three*.
RAY: Twenty-three, and she's not married.
MIKE: Pleased to meet you Patty.
PATTY: Pleased to meet you Mike . . . Oh look! There's Sam. Sam . . . Sam . . . over here.
SAM: Oh, hi Patty! What's going on here?
PATTY: Sam, let me introduce Ray and Mike.
SAM: Hi.
RAY: Pleased to meet you.
MIKE: Hello.
PATTY: But we don't know anything about Ray, do we? What do *you* do Ray?
RAY: Well, it's a bit difficult to explain . . .

ANNOUNCER: Activity Book Unit **5**. Listen.

(*Footsteps down a street. Car approaches, slows down and stops with engine still running.*)
INSPECTOR: Hello Charlie!
CHARLIE: Hello.
INSPECTOR: Charlie, it's me! Inspector Bender.
CHARLIE: Oh, hello Inspector.
INSPECTOR: Charlie, come here.
CHARLIE: Well?
INSPECTOR: Hello, Charlie. Now then, where were you at nine o'clock yesterday evening?
CHARLIE: At home.
INSPECTOR: At home. Who was with you?
CHARLIE: My wife, and the two children.
INSPECTOR: How nice. What about ten o'clock? Where were you at ten o'clock?
CHARLIE: I was . . . er . . . well . . .
INSPECTOR: Come on Charlie. Where were you?
CHARLIE: At a disco.
INSPECTOR: You were at a disco?!
CHARLIE: Yes, I was.
INSPECTOR: Who with?
CHARLIE: Well . . .
INSPECTOR: Who with Charlie? Who were you with?
CHARLIE: Your wife.
INSPECTOR: Your wife?
CHARLIE: No Inspector, *your* wife.
INSPECTOR: My wife! Now you listen to me Charlie, I've . . .

ANNOUNCER: Activity Book Unit **6**. Listen.

(*Party noises.*)
JUDITH: George!
GEORGE: Yes?
JUDITH: Look at the time! It's twelve o'clock.
GEORGE: Twelve o'clock! Come on Judith . . .
RACHEL: Here are the hats and coats everybody. Whose hat is this?
GEORGE: Oh thanks, Rachel, that's mine.
RACHEL: Yours George?
GEORGE: Yes, mine. Why?

RACHEL: I don't like it very much!
GEORGE: Oh, come on, Rachel.
RACHEL: Here's a coat! Whose coat is this?
JUDITH: Oh, that's mine . . . Thanks . . . oh dear! Where are my gloves?
RACHEL: Oh Judith, aren't they in your coat?
JUDITH: No . . . oh, where are they?
GEORGE: Aren't those yours?
JUDITH: Where?
GEORGE: There . . . on the table.
JUDITH: Oh yes . . . thanks.
GEORGE: Rachel, thanks for the party. It was lovely.
RACHEL: Not at all George. Come again.
GEORGE: We will. Come on, Judith.
JUDITH: Thanks very much, Rachel. Lovely party. Goodbye.
RACHEL: Bye! Bye!
GEORGE: } Goodbye!
JUDITH: }

ANNOUNCER: Activity Book Unit **7**. Listen.

(*Phone rings*)
JOHN: Richard Travel. Good morning, can I help you?
MAGGIE: Yes, please, I want to book a flight.
JOHN: Certainly, madam. Where to?
MAGGIE: Madrid. Madrid, Spain.
JOHN: A flight to Madrid. When do you want to travel?
MAGGIE: Oh, um, 15th January, and then I want a flight to Acapulco on 27th February, returning to London on 10th March.
JOHN: So that's Madrid on the fifteenth, Acapulco on the twenty-seventh of next month and you want to come back to London on the tenth of March.
MAGGIE: That's right.
JOHN: Well, yes, that seems to be possible. Do you want first or tourist class?
MAGGIE: Oh, tourist, please.
JOHN: Thank you, madam. Can I have your name and address?
MAGGIE: Yes, of course. My name is Maggie Shore and the address is 56 Bridge Street, London W2.
JOHN: This Bridge Street? I'm in Bridge Street here.
MAGGIE: Yes, that's right. And one more thing . . .
JOHN: Yes?
MAGGIE: Can I have an extra seat?
JOHN: Yes, madam, of course. What name is it for the extra ticket?
MAGGIE: John Richard.
JOHN: But that's my name!
MAGGIE: Yes it is. The ticket is for you.
JOHN: But . . . but . . . who are you?
MAGGIE: I'm Maggie! I work in the office opposite your travel agency. Look out of your window.
JOHN: Oh! Hello, Maggie.
MAGGIE: Hello, John. Pleased to meet you.

ANNOUNCER: Activity Book Unit **8**. Listen.

CHAT SHOW HOST: Hello, hello, hello, and welcome to another edition of 'Today', the programme where we talk to the beautiful and the famous. In tonight's programme, ladies and gentlemen, we are going to talk to the singer Bart Scott. Ladies and gentlemen, please welcome Bart Scott.
(*Studio applause*)
BART: Hello . . . hi . . . thanks, thanks a lot.
CSH: Bart, thank you for coming here tonight. Now tell us something about *you*!
BART: Of course . . . ask me some questions.
CSH: Well, to start with, where are you from, originally?
BART: Well, I'm English, but I was born in Bombay.
CSH: Bombay, India?
BART: Yes, that's right. My mother and father were there for ten years.
CSH: And do you like India?
BART: Do I like India? Well yes, I think so.
CSH: And, er . . . what about . . . er . . . curry, Indian curry? Do you like Indian curry?
BART: I don't know. I've never tried it.
CSH: Oh, really? Why not?
BART: Well, I was only one year old when I left India and came to England.
CSH: So you live in England now?
BART: Oh no! I live in New York.
CSH: Oh . . . why do you live in New York?
BART: Because I prefer it to English cities. It's exciting, there's lots to do. And I just love the people.
CSH: One last question, Bart. What's your favourite kind of music?
BART: That's easy! *My* music!
CSH: Oh . . . er . . . yes, of course. Ladies and gentlemen Bart Scott.
(*Studio applause*)

ANNOUNCER: Activity Book Unit **9**. Listen.

(*Knock on door*)
Doctor (female): Come in . . . come in.
Ah, hello. Please take a seat.
ANGELA: Thank you, doctor.
DOCTOR: You're Angela Stansgate, aren't you?
ANGELA: Yes, I am.
DOCTOR: Well Angela, how can I help you?
ANGELA: Doctor, I have this pain.
DOCTOR: Where?
ANGELA: In my head . . . I mean I have a lot of headaches.
DOCTOR: I see . . . Let me ask you some questions. What do you do?
ANGELA: I'm a teacher.
DOCTOR: A teacher . . . umm . . . do you smoke?
ANGELA: Yes, I do. About thirty cigarettes a day.
DOCTOR: I see. And what about exercise? Do you take any exercise? Do you play tennis? Do you swim?
ANGELA: No. You see I don't have the time. I work hard and I have a lot to do . . .
DOCTOR: Now listen Miss Stansgate, you've got a problem. Actually you've got two problems. You smoke and you don't take exercise.
ANGELA: Yes.
DOCTOR: So there are three things you must do . . .
DOCTOR: One, stop smoking. Don't have any cigarettes at all. Two, take exercise two or three times a week. Swim, run or play tennis. All right?
ANGELA: Yes, doctor.
DOCTOR: And three . . . take an aspirin every morning.
ANGELA: (*Groans*)

ANNOUNCER: Activity Book Unit **10**. Listen.
One. George Hayes goes to the 'Find Your Partner' Agency.

SMOTHER: Good morning! Good morning! Come in, come in.

HAYES: Er, thank you . . . good morning.
SMOTHER: Good morning, sit down, please, sit down. Now then, what is your name?
HAYES: Hayes, George Hayes.
SMOTHER: Well — George — tell me about your ideal wife!
HAYES: Oh . . . er, what do I say?
SMOTHER: Well, do you like tall women, short women, old women, young women? We've got all of them you know!
HAYES: Well I like short women. Yes, my ideal wife is short. I'm short you know.
SMOTHER: Yes, I can see that.
HAYES: And . . . er . . . my ideal wife has brown eyes . . . and, well, a happy face.
SMOTHER: A happy face?
HAYES: Yes.
SMOTHER: Yes. Well now . . . short woman, brown eyes . . . happy face.

ANNOUNCER: Two. Listen.

SMOTHER: Hello! Hello! Come in. Sit down!
ORCHARD: Thank you.
SMOTHER: And you are?
ORCHARD: Fenella Orchard. I want a husband.
SMOTHER: I see. Tell me about your ideal husband.
ORCHARD: Well, my ideal husband is tall and thin . . .
SMOTHER: Tall and thin . . . . .
ORCHARD: With blond . . . no, grey hair and blue eyes.
SMOTHER: Yes, well they all want one of those.

ANNOUNCER: Three. Listen.

SMOTHER: And what's your name?
RICHARDS: Stella. Stella Richards.
SMOTHER: Hello Stella.
RICHARDS: Hello.
SMOTHER: Well, here at 'Find Your Partner' we're ready to help you find your ideal husband. What does he look like, Stella?
RICHARDS: Mmm . . . well . . . can he have a beard?
SMOTHER: A beard?
RICHARDS: And glasses.
SMOTHER: And glasses.
RICHARDS: And he'd better be short.
SMOTHER: O.K. So your ideal husband would be a short man with a beard and glasses.
RICHARDS: Yes.

ANNOUNCER: Four. Listen.

SMOTHER: Good morning!
Welcome to 'Find Your Partner'
Er . . . come in . . . sit down.
WINTERTON: Thank you young man.
SMOTHER: Please . . . *please* sit down, Mr . . . er . . .?
WINTERTON: Winterton. Albert Winterton.
SMOTHER: Yes, Mr Winterton?
WINTERTON: I'm looking for a new wife.
SMOTHER: You're looking for a new wife.
WINTERTON: Yes. I want a tall, thin one with blue eyes and blond hair.
SMOTHER: Er . . . yes . . . a tall thin woman with blue eyes and blond hair. Excuse me, Mr Winterton but . . . er . . . how old are you?
WINTERTON: A hundred and four.

ANNOUNCER: Activity Book Unit **11**. Listen.

(*Knocking on door*)
MANAGER: Come in!
PEABODY: Thank you . . . er . . . good morning.
MANAGER: Hello. Please take a seat Miss . . . ?
PEABODY: Peabody. Brenda Peabody.
MANAGER: Ah yes, Miss Peabody. Now then, I've got a few questions . . . Let's see. Can you type?
PEABODY: Type?
MANAGER: Yes. Can you type?
PEABODY: No. No, I can't type.
MANAGER: I see. What about shorthand?
PEABODY: Shorthand?
MANAGER: Yes, shorthand. Can you take shorthand?
PEABODY: I don't know. I've never tried.
MANAGER: So you can't take shorthand and you can't type. What can you do, may I ask?
PEABODY: Well, I can play the piano and the guitar.
MANAGER: Play the piano and the guitar?
PEABODY: Yes, and I can dance and sing.
MANAGER: Miss Peabody what are you doing here?
PEABODY: I want a job. I want to work here.
MANAGER: But Miss Peabody, you can't take shorthand and you can't even type!
PEABODY: No, of course I can't. I'm an actress.
MANAGER: But I want a secretary.
PEABODY: Is this the City Theatre?
MANAGER: No, of course it isn't. It's the City Bank. The City Theatre is in the next street opposite the hospital.

ANNOUNCER: Activity Book Unit **12**. Listen.

TERRY: Hello . . . Hello . . . and welcome to all of our viewers down there on earth. I hope you can see the pictures we are sending you from the Nasa Space Station. We are here in space orbiting the earth, and from this window I can see the United States. . . . My name is Terry Duggan and I'm a Reporter for SBC Television. Right now I'm talking to Bud Samson, an astronaut here on the space station but it's rather difficult because we cannot stand up or sit down! We're all weightless here, and . . . Bud? Bud Samson? Where are you? Oh, there you are. Bud, what is life like on the space station?
BUD: It's fine. I like it a lot.
TERRY: But what do you do here all day?
BUD: The usual things, I guess. I mean I always have breakfast at 6 o'clock, and I usually have a shower before that.
TERRY: A shower? That's impossible!
BUD: No, it isn't. It's great fun!
TERRY: I see. What else do you do?
BUD: Well . . . we often talk to our families back on earth. We watch old movies . . . that kind of thing.
TERRY: What about hobbies? Do you have any hobbies?
BUD: I do, yes. I play chess.
TERRY: Do you play well?
BUD: Not too badly.
TERRY: That's interesting. One last question. What's the food like here?
BUD: Not very good. We rarely cook anything. We just eat food substitutes.
TERRY: What are food substitutes?
BUD: Little green pills! But don't worry. We do cook sometimes.
TERRY: Oh, what do you cook? What's your favourite kind of food?

BUD: Spaghetti.
TERRY: Spaghetti? Here?
BUD: Yes, of course. Weightless spaghetti. Look over there. That piece of spaghetti is still here and we cooked it yesterday morning!

ANNOUNCER: Activity Book Unit **13**. Listen.

GEORGE: Hello.
OPERATOR: Hello. Is that Mr George Whitney?
GEORGE: Yes.
OPERATOR: I have a call for you from Athens, Greece, from Mrs Whitney. Will you pay for the call?
GEORGE: Yes, I will.
OPERATOR: Go ahead please caller.
JUDITH: Hello! Hello! George!
GEORGE: Hello, Judith.
JUDITH: Hello . . . Hello.
GEORGE: Hello, dear.
JUDITH: George. How are you?
GEORGE: I'm feeling terrible. I've got a headache and Tony's upstairs playing his guitar and singing at the top of his voice.
JUDITH: Oh poor George. What about Jane and Martin? How are they?
GEORGE: Well Jane's in her room doing her homework.
JUDITH: Good for Jane!
GEORGE: And Martin's in the kitchen washing the dishes.
JUDITH: In the kitchen?
GEORGE: Yes. He's washing the dishes.
JUDITH: I don't believe it.
GEORGE: It's true!
JUDITH: What about you? What are you doing?
GEORGE: I'm talking to you! Actually I'm trying to watch the television. There's a good programme on so I'll say goodbye.
JUDITH: But George! Don't you want to ask me any questions? Don't you want to hear about Greece?
GEORGE: Er . . . Yes, of course. What's Greece like, dear?
(*Buzzing on the line*)
Hello . . . Judith . . . are you there? Can you hear me Judith?
OPERATOR: I'm afraid we've lost the connection from Athens, sir.
GEORGE: Oh no!

ANNOUNCER: Activity Book Unit **14**. Listen.

MAGGIE: Oh this is fantastic! It's an incredible restaurant.
JOHN: Yes. It's the most famous restaurant in Acapulco.
MAGGIE: This is a wonderful holiday. I'm enjoying myself so much.
JOHN: I'm glad. Now then, would you like avocado vinaigrette to start with?
MAGGIE: I'd prefer some soup if they've got any.
JOHN: Let me ask. Waiter!
WAITER: Yes, sir.
JOHN: Have you got any soup? I can't see any on the menu.
WAITER: Yes, sir. Of course. There it is, right there.
JOHN: Oh yes. Thank you. Well Maggie, what would you like? Vegetable soup? Gazpacho? Mushroom soup?
MAGGIE: I'm going to have mushroom soup I think, and then the steak.
JOHN: O.K. Waiter, can we have two mushroom soups and two steaks.
WAITER: Very good, sir.
MAGGIE: Oh John. Look at those men. They've all got musical instruments and those big Mexican hats.
JOHN: Yes, Maggie. That's a Mariachi Band.
MAGGIE: They're coming to our table.
JOHN: Yes, Maggie.
MUSICIAN: Good evening senorita. A very happy birthday to you.
MAGGIE: John! How did you know?
JOHN: Today is the ninth of March. It's in your passport.
(*Music*)
JOHN: Maggie, just one more thing.
MAGGIE: Yes, John?
JOHN: I've got a question for you.
MAGGIE: Yes, John?
JOHN: Will you . . . that is . . . can I . . . could I . . . would you . . . ?
MAGGIE: What John?
JOHN: Will you marry me?
MAGGIE: Yes, of course I will.

ANNOUNCER: Activity Book Unit **15**. Listen.

WOMAN: 2674583. Hello!
MAN: Hello. I'm ringing about the house. I saw the advertisement in the newspaper.
WOMAN: Yes . . . what can I tell you?
MAN: Well, how many bedrooms are there?
WOMAN: Fifteen.
MAN: Fifteen! Good heavens! Is there much land with the house?
WOMAN: No, not much really. Only about forty-five acres.
MAN: Forty-five acres! That's a fantastic amount. What about bathrooms? How many bathrooms has the house got?
WOMAN: I'm not really sure. I think there are two on the ground floor and three upstairs . . . yes, that's right.
MAN: I can't believe this! It's absolutely fantastic! Fifteen bedrooms, five bathrooms, forty-five acres of land! My wife's going to love it!
WOMAN: Well don't forget the swimming pools.
MAN: Swimming pools? Did you say pools?
WOMAN: Why yes, of course. We've got two here. One for the children and one for us.
MAN: And how many rooms are there altogether?
WOMAN: Oh, about forty-five . . . No, forty-four.
MAN: And that's all for ninety thousand dollars? I just can't believe it! Forty-four rooms, two swimming pools, ninety thousand dollars. It's fantastic! My wife's going to . . .
WOMAN: It's not ninety thousand.
MAN: What?
WOMAN: It's not ninety thousand. There was a mistake in the newspaper. They forgot a zero. It's nine hundred thousand! Hello . . . Hello . . . is anybody there?

ANNOUNCER: Activity Book Unit **16**. Listen.

INTERVIEWER: I'm here at the Nasa space centre at Cape Kennedy. I'm talking to the director of the space shuttle programme, Ernest B. Gold. Good morning, Mr Gold.
GOLD: Hello.
INTERVIEWER: Mr Gold, last week you had a problem with the shuttle, I believe.
GOLD: That is correct. The launch of this mission was cancelled — postponed.
INTERVIEWER: Why was that?

GOLD: We had a fault in the number three computer system I'm afraid. But it's all right now.

INTERVIEWER: So when is the shuttle going to lift off?

GOLD: Lift-off is at oh nine fifteen and the shuttle will reach the space station at fourteen hundred hours.

INTERVIEWER: Who's going to be in the crew tomorrow?

GOLD: It's the same crew as before: that's the three men, Allen, Long and Terelli; and one female member of the crew, Tracey Allwright.

INTERVIEWER: And what are they going to do on this mission Mr Gold?

GOLD: Well the main objective of the mission is, of course, to deliver supplies to the space station. But Allen and Long are also going to study radiation levels and take more photographs of the moon.

INTERVIEWER: Mr Gold, why is Steve Terelli going on this mission?

GOLD: Well he's an experienced astronaut and he's a good Italian cook.

INTERVIEWER: Cook! Just what is the shuttle going to deliver to the space station?

GOLD: Supplies.

INTERVIEWER: What supplies, exactly?

GOLD: Er ..... well, a lot of spaghetti.

INTERVIEWER: Spaghetti!

GOLD: Yes, it's Bud Samson's favourite food and he's an astronaut at the space station.

ANNOUNCER: Activity Book Unit **17**. Listen.

POLICEMAN: Now, Mrs Jones, can you tell me what happened?

MRS JONES: I can't really remember, you know. It was terrible! Terrible!

POLICEMAN: Yes I know, but you must try to remember. Let's start from the beginning. Where were you?

MRS JONES: Well, I was in the chemist's. I bought some aspirin for my headache. You see I often have headaches . . .

POLICEMAN: So you were in the chemist's. What did you see?

MRS JONES: Some men drove up to the bank in a car. It was a big, red car and very fast, I think.

POLICEMAN: How many men?

MRS JONES: Three. There were three men. Two young ones, and an older man with dark glasses.

POLICEMAN: What did the three men do?

MRS JONES: The two young men ran into the bank.

POLICEMAN: And what about the other man? What did he do?

MRS JONES: He stayed outside the bank, by the door, the entrance. He watched the street. Waiting for the police, I imagine.

POLICEMAN: I'm sure! What happened then?

MRS JONES: Well there were some noises . . . bang, bang. Guns, I think. The two men ran out of the bank with guns in their hands. They got into their car and the older man — the man with glasses — started to run to the car too.

POLICEMAN: And did he get there?

MRS JONES: Oh no. Poor man. There was a shot — bang! — from the bank and the man fell down. He died right there, in front of the bank.

POLICEMAN: What about the other two? Did they drive away?

MRS JONES: Oh yes, and very fast.

POLICEMAN: And what did you do, Mrs Jones?

MRS JONES: Well you can imagine how horrid it was! I suddenly felt dizzy and I fainted.

POLICEMAN: Oh dear, I'm sorry. Are you feeling all right now?

MRS JONES: Oh, yes. Yes, thank you. That lovely sergeant of yours — the tall one with the beard — gave me a cup of tea. I feel *much* better.

ANNOUNCER: Activity Book Unit **18**. Listen.

CHAIRMAN: . . . And next week we are going to hold our annual meeting at the town hall . . .

JANICE: Hello, hello, everybody!

CHAIRMAN: Janice! Where have you been? You're late!

JANICE: I'm sorry.

CHAIRMAN: You're always late! What happened this time?

JANICE: Well I put all my things into my briefcase, and I was just about to leave the house when there was a knock at the door.

CHAIRMAN: Yes?

JANICE: And it was the milkman who wanted some money. So I paid him and he put two bottles of milk on the kitchen table and then he went.

CHAIRMAN: Yes, Janice, go on.

JANICE: Well, and then I put on my coat, went out of the door and closed it. And there was a terrible crash!

CHAIRMAN: What was it?

JANICE: It was Marmalade.

CHAIRMAN: Who or what is Marmalade?

JANICE: Marmalade is my cat and he had knocked a bottle of milk off the table. So I had to clean the floor, and then I ran out of the house, and got on my bicycle to come here.

CHAIRMAN: Well now you're here you can .....

JANICE: And in the High Street a small child ran in front of me and I fell off my bicycle and a policeman helped me off the ground and I picked up my bicycle and here I am.

CHAIRMAN: Good. Now where is your report?

JANICE: In my briefcase.

CHAIRMAN: And where is your briefcase?

JANICE: I left it at home!

ANNOUNCER: Activity Book Unit **19**. Listen.

JO: Hello Anne.

ANNE: Jo! Hi! How are you?

JO: Oh, not too bad.

ANNE: What are you doing these days?

JO: I'm working with an all-woman parachute team.

ANNE: A parachute team?

JO: Yes, it's really fantastic! Would you like to come along this weekend? You could learn how to jump!

ANNE: I can't, I'm afraid. I have to train for next month's race.

JO: But you train every day. This is special!

ANNE: I know. Jo. I'm sure it is. But I want to win the marathon next month and that means I have to run ten miles every day — including weekends.

JO: Oh please come, Anne.

ANNE: No, really, I can't.

JO: You don't want to, do you?

ANNE: It's not that. I'm a marathon runner. I have to train.

JO: But you'd like to make a parachute jump wouldn't you?

ANNE: To be honest Jo, no I wouldn't. I really would not like to jump out of an aeroplane at 3,000 feet. It's a crazy thing to do. I would be terrified!

JO: Yes, actually I'm terrified too.

ANNE: But you said . . .

JO: Yes, I know I did. I like the training sessions. But tomorrow's my first real jump!

ANNOUNCER: Activity Book Unit **20**. Listen.

MICK: Hey Gerald, how did you get on? Did you like the exam?

GERALD: No, I didn't. I thought it was terrible.

MICK: Oh, come on! It wasn't that bad. Which questions did you do?

GERALD: I did the first one — you know, the one about the uses of computers in the modern world.

MICK: Yes, I did that one too.

GERALD: And I did number 4 — about the cost of medicine. But I got into a terrible mess.

MICK: You didn't do the one about the price of oil did you?

GERALD: What, you mean question 3?

MICK: Yes.

GERALD: Yes, I did question 3. That's just the problem.

MICK: Why?

GERALD: Well, I didn't finish it. I think I failed.

MICK: No, you didn't. I'm sure you didn't. You can come to the party tonight, can't you?

GERALD: I don't think so. I'm not feeling very cheerful.

(*Judy comes through door*)

JUDY: Hello Mick, how did you get on?

MICK: Not too badly. What about you?

JUDY: Well I did question 2 — about car production. That was difficult. But I enjoyed questions 3 and 4 — the ones about oil and medicine.

MICK: Why didn't you answer the one about jobs and production — you studied that.

JUDY: What, number 5?

MICK: Yes.

JUDY: You didn't do that one did you?

MICK: Yes, actually, I did.

JUDY: You're crazy. It was impossible. Anyway, I'm going now. See you!

MICK: Hey, you're going to be at the party, aren't you?

JUDY: Yes, of course. Bye.

GERALD: Who was that?

MICK: 'That' was Judy. Don't you know her?

GERALD: I think I've seen her before. But I didn't know her name.

MICK: Anyway, what about the party? Do you think you'll come?

GERALD: Yes . . . yes, I think I will now!